Democrat
2020 Gun Control Plan

Gun Violence Prevention and
Community Safety Act of 2020
H.R. 5717

LARGE PRINT EDITION

116th CONGRESS 2d Session

Thirteen Colony Press

Thirteen Colony Press
c/o Sastrugi Press LLC
PO Box 1297, Jackson, WY 83001, United States
www.sastrugipress.com

CIP data available
U.S. Congress House of Representatives
Democrat 2020 Gun Control Plan / U.S. House of Representatives —1st United States edition

p. cm.

1. Civics 2. Politics 3. Government
The 2020 Democrat-controlled House of Representatives has submitted H.R. 5717 for Congressional consideration which dramatically changes the firearms ownership and sale landscape of the United States.

Thirteen Colony Press is an imprint of Sastrugi Press LLC.

Printed in the United States of America when bought in the United States of America.
10 9 8 7 6 5 4 3 2 1
Sastrugi Press
00218

CONTENTS

H.R. 5717 GUN VIOLENCE PREVENTION AND COMMUNITY SAFETY ACT OF 2020
Overview

This proposed gun legislation will:

- Create an unelected commission that determines safety standards.
- Requires firearms and ammunition dealers to submit to filing a plan and having be accepted.
- Makes firearms manufacturers liable for the action of criminal gun users regardless of how to criminal came to possess the firearm.
- Makes it illegal to import, sell, manufacture, transfer, or possess, in or affecting interstate or foreign commerce, a semiautomatic assault weapon.

Sections of interest in the proposed bill for the reader

Title I
Sec. 101

- Requires a license for any firearms or ammunition ownership or purchase
- Requires a written and hands-on test and a photograph of the purchaser
- Establishes a database of all buyers of all guns and ammunition
- Requires registration of all firearms

Sec 303: Increases the age of ownership to 21, even though 18-year-olds may join the military and use military-grade weapons

Sec 304: Requires government-acceptable storage requirement for all firearms owners. Guns must be locked up and disabled at all times if anyone who can access them doesn't have a firearms license.

Title IV: Creates Red Flag confiscation law (Extreme Risk Protection)
- Circumvents the 4th amendment
- The text suggests home inspections as deemed necessary

Title V: Bans "Assault weapons"
Sec 512: Limits magazine capacity to 10 rounds or less. Is unclear about semi-automatic pistols now being classified as assault weapons
Sec 515: Make creating firearm models illegal

Subtitle B
Completely ban silencers and mufflers
Title VI
Sec 934: Selling two or more firearms is now classified as firearms trafficking. Restricts everyone to one purchase per month regardless of source (store, private, etc.). Make people who privately sell firearms liable for the action of the purchaser.

Title VII: Firearms dealers and ammunition vendors
- Require gun dealers to submit a security plan for

certification which can be rejected

- Owners must report a theft or loss of a firearm within 48 hours or be fined $1,000
- Create an annual security plan compliance certification with a $5,000 fine
- Require gun dealers to submit to annual inspections by the federal attorney general's office
- Imposes up to a $20,000 fine is the inspector decides they dont' like what the gun dealer has done
- Every gun and ammunition dealer must keep a record of every firearm and box of ammunition sold and maintain that record indefinitely (forever).

Title VIII: Sec 803 New, burdensom tax increases
- *Taxes firearms at 30%*
- *Taxes ammunition at 50%*

Bill Cosponsors

Rep. Kennedy, Joseph P., III [D-MA-4]*
01/30/2020
Rep. Quigley, Mike [D-IL-5]*   01/30/2020
Rep. Brown, Anthony G. [D-MD-4]*   01/30/2020
Rep. Morelle, Joseph D. [D-NY-25]*   01/30/2020
Rep. DeLauro, Rosa L. [D-CT-3]* 01/30/2020
Rep. Maloney, Carolyn B. [D-NY-12]*   01/30/2020
Rep. Keating, William R. [D-MA-9]*   01/30/2020
Rep. Lynch, Stephen F. [D-MA-8]*   01/30/2020
Rep. Moulton, Seth [D-MA-6]*   01/30/2020
Rep. Pressley, Ayanna [D-MA-7]*01/30/2020
Rep. Trahan, Lori [D-MA-3]*   01/30/2020
Rep. McGovern, James P. [D-MA-2]*   01/30/2020
Rep. Davis, Danny K. [D-IL-7]*   01/30/2020
Rep. Neal, Richard E. [D-MA-1]* 01/30/2020
Rep. Clark, Katherine M. [D-MA-5]*   01/30/2020
Rep. Pascrell, Bill, Jr. [D-NJ-9]*   01/30/2020
Rep. Engel, Eliot L. [D-NY-16]   02/04/2020
Rep. Norton, Eleanor Holmes [D-DC-At Large]
03/10/2020

H.R. 5717 GUN VIOLENCE PREVENTION AND COMMUNITY SAFETY ACT OF 2020
Summary

Gun Violence Prevention and Community Safety Act of 2020

Introduced in House (01/30/2020)

This bill makes various changes to the federal framework governing the sale, transfer, and possession of firearms and ammunition. Among other things, the bill does the following:

- generally requires individuals to obtain a license to purchase, acquire, or possess a firearm or ammunition;
- raises the minimum age—from 18 years to 21 years—to purchase firearms and ammunition;
- establishes new background check requirements for firearm transfers between private parties;
- requires law enforcement agencies to be notified following a firearms-related background check that results in a denial;
- creates a statutory process for a family or household member to petition a court for an extreme risk protection order to remove firearms from an individual who poses a risk of committing violence;
- restricts the import, sale, manufacture, transfer, or possession of semiautomatic assault weapons and large capacity ammunition feeding devices;
- restricts the manufacture, sale, transfer, purchase, or receipt of ghost guns (i.e., guns without serial numbers);

- makes trafficking in firearms a stand-alone criminal offense;
- requires federally licensed gun dealers to submit and annually certify compliance with a security plan to detect and deter firearm theft;
- removes limitations on the civil liability of gun manufacturers;
- allows the Consumer Product Safety Commission to issue safety standards for firearms and firearm components;
- establishes a community violence intervention grant program; and
- promotes research on firearms safety and gun violence prevention.

H.R. 5717 GUN VIOLENCE PREVENTION AND COMMUNITY SAFETY ACT OF 2020
Complete Text

116th CONGRESS
2d Session
H. R. 5717

To end the epidemic of gun violence and build saf-
er communities by strengthening Federal firearms
laws and supporting gun violence research, intervention, and prevention initiatives.

IN THE HOUSE OF REPRESENTATIVES
January 30, 2020
Mr. Johnson of Georgia (for himself, Mr. Kennedy,
Mr. Quigley, Mr. Brown of Maryland, Mr. Morelle,
Ms. DeLauro, Mrs. Carolyn B. Maloney of New
York, Mr. Keating, Mr. Lynch, Mr. Moulton, Ms.
Pressley, Mrs. Trahan, Mr. McGovern, Mr. Danny
K. Davis of Illinois, Mr. Neal, Ms. Clark of Massa-
chusetts, and Mr. Pascrell) introduced the following
bill; which was referred to the Committee on the
Judiciary, and in addition to the Committees on
Energy and Commerce, and Ways and Means, for a
period to be subsequently determined by the Speak-
er, in each case for consideration of such provisions
as fall within the jurisdiction of the committee con-
cerned

A BILL
To end the epidemic of gun violence and build saf-
er communities by strengthening Federal firearms
laws and supporting gun violence research, inter-

vention, and prevention initiatives.

Be it enacted by the Senate and House of Representatives of the United States of America in Congress assembled,

SECTION 1. SHORT TITLE; TABLE OF CONTENTS.
(a) Short Title.—This Act may be cited as the "Gun Violence Prevention and Community Safety Act of 2020".

(b) Table Of Contents.—The table of contents for this Act is as follows:

arms.
Sec. 516. Prohibition on possession of certain firearm accessories.
Subtitle B—Firearm Silencers And Mufflers Ban

Sec. 521. Definition.
Sec. 522. Restrictions on firearm silencers and firearm mufflers.
Sec. 523. Penalties.
Sec. 524. Effective date.

TITLE VI—FIREARM TRAFFICKING

Sec. 601. Prohibition against multiple firearm sales or purchases.
Sec. 602. Increased penalties for making knowingly false statements in connection with firearms.
Sec. 603. Retention of records.
Sec. 604. Revised definition.
Sec. 605. Firearms trafficking.

TITLE VII—DEALER REFORM

Sec. 701. Gun shop security measures.
Sec. 702. Inspections.
Sec. 703. Employee background checks.
Sec. 704. Gun store thefts.
Sec. 705. Civil enforcement.
Sec. 706. No effect on State laws governing dealing in firearms.
Sec. 707. Lost and stolen reporting requirement.
Sec. 708. Report on implementation.

TITLE I—FIREARM LICENSING

SEC. 101. LICENSE TO OWN FIREARMS AND AMMUNITION.

(a) In General.—Chapter 44 of title 18, United States Code, is amended by adding at the end the following:

"§ 932. License to own firearms and ammunition

"(a) In General.—Except otherwise provided in this section, it shall be unlawful for any individual who is not licensed under this section to knowingly purchase, acquire, or possess a firearm or ammunition.

"(b) Eligibility.—An individual shall be eligible to receive a license under this section if the individual—

"(1) has attained 21 years of age; and

"(2) has completed training in firearms safety, including—

"(A) a written test, to demonstrate knowledge of applicable firearms laws;

"(B) hands-on testing, including firing testing, to demonstrate safe use of a firearm;

"(C) as part of the process for applying for such a license—

"(i) has submitted to a background investigation and criminal history check of the individual, including a background check using the National Instant Criminal Background Check System, to ensure the individual is not prohibited from possessing a firearm under subsection (g) or (n) of section 922; and

"(ii) has submitted a photograph of the individual;
"(D) has not been determined by a court, in accordance with subsection (c)(5), to be unsuitable to be issued a Federal firearm owner's license; and

"(E) is not otherwise prohibited by Federal, State, Tribal, or local law from possessing a firearm.
"(c) Establishment Of Federal Firearm Owner's License.—
"(1) IN GENERAL.—The Attorney General shall issue a Federal firearm owner's license to any individual who is eligible under subsection (b).
"(2) ISSUANCE OF LICENSE OR NOTICE OF DENIAL.—Not later than 40 days after the date on which an individual submits an application for a Federal firearm owner's license under this section, the Attorney General shall—

"(A) determine whether the individual is eligible to possess a license under this section; and

"(B) based on the determination under subparagraph (A)—

"(i) issue a Federal firearm owner's license to the individual; or "(ii) provide written notice to the individual of—

"(I) the determination that the individual is ineligible to possess such a license based on the requirements described in subsection (b), which shall include an explanation for the determination; or

"(II) a petition filed under paragraph (5).

"(3) EXPIRATION.—A Federal firearm owner's license issued under this section shall expire on the date that is 10 years after the date on which the license was issued.

"(4) RENEWAL OF LICENSE.—

"(A) IN GENERAL.—A Federal firearm owner's license issued under this section may be renewed at the end of the 10-year period described in paragraph (3).

"(B) REQUIREMENTS.—The process for renewal of a Federal firearm owner's license under subparagraph (A) shall include—

"(i) an up-to-date background investigation and criminal history check of the individual; and

"(ii) a recent photograph of the individual.

"(C) ISSUANCE OF RENEWAL OR NOTICE OF DENIAL.—Not later than 40 days after the date on which an individual submits an application for a renewal of a Federal firearm owner's license under this paragraph, the Attorney General shall—

"(i) issue a renewed Federal firearm owner's license to the individual; and

"(ii) provide written notice to the individual of—

"(I) the determination that the individual is ineligible to possess such a license based on the requirements described in subsection (b), which shall include an explanation for the determination; or

"(II) a petition filed under paragraph (5).

"(5) ATF DETERMINATION OF UNSUITABILITY.—

"(A) IN GENERAL.—The Director of the Bureau of Alcohol, Tobacco, Firearms and Explosives may file a petition, which shall contain a written statement of the reasons supporting the request required under subparagraph (C), in an appropriate district court of the United States to request that—

"(i) an individual who has applied for a Federal firearm owner's license, or renewal thereof, under this section be denied the request for such license; or

"(ii) a previously issued Federal firearm owner's license be suspended or revoked.

"(B) NOTICE.—Any petition filed under subparagraph (A) shall include written notice to the individual who requested, or is in possession of, the Federal firearm owner's license, as the case may be, describing the facts and circumstances justifying the petition.

"(C) HEARING.—Not later than 90 days after the date on which a petition is filed under subparagraph (A), the court shall conduct a hearing.

"(D) FACTORS TO DETERMINE UNSUITABILITY.—Not later than 15 days after the date on which a hearing is conducted under subparagraph (C), the court shall find that an individual is unsuitable to possess a Federal firearm owner's license if, based on a preponderance of the evidence, there exists—

"(i) reliable, articulable, and credible information that the individual has exhibited or engaged in behavior to suggest the individual could potentially create a risk to public safety; or

"(ii) other existing factors that suggest that the individual could potentially create a risk to public safety.

"(E) NOTICE OF DETERMINATION.—If a court finds an individual is unsuitable to possess a Federal firearm owner's license, the court shall notify the applicant in writing, setting forth the specific reasons for such determination.

"(6) REVIEW.—A determination of the Director of Bureau of Alcohol, Tobacco, Firearms and Explosives or a district court of the United States under this subparagraph may be appealed to the appropriate court of the United States.

"(d) Exceptions.—

"(1) PREVIOUSLY POSSESSED FIREARMS.—Subsection (a) shall not apply to the possession of any firearm or ammunition by an individual who otherwise lawfully possessed the firearm or ammunition under Federal law on the date on which the Attorney General begins issuing Federal firearm owner's licenses under this section.

"(2) STATE LICENSES.—

"(A) IN GENERAL.—Subsection (a) shall not apply to an individual in a State if the Attorney General determines that the State—

"(i) has in effect a process for issuing a State firearm owner's license to eligible individuals in the State that is substantially similar to the requirements of subsection (b); and

"(ii) provides to the Attorney General real-time validity information relating to firearm owner's licenses issued by the State, for inclusion in the database described in section (f).

"(B) PUBLICATION OF LIST OF QUALIFYING STATES.—

"(i) IN GENERAL.—Not later than 2 years after the date of enactment of the Gun Violence Prevention and Community Safety Act of 2020, the Attorney General shall publish a list of States that have in effect a process described in subparagraph (A).

"(ii) UPDATED LIST.—The Attorney General shall update the list described in clause (i) immediately upon determining that a State should be included on or removed from the list.

"(3) LICENSED DEALERS, MANUFACTURERS, AND IMPORTERS.—Subsection (a) shall not apply to an individual who is a licensed dealer, licensed manufacturer, or licensed importer.

"(4) AGENCIES AND LAW ENFORCEMENT OFFICERS.—

"(A) IN GENERAL.—Subsection (a) shall not apply to—

"(i) the importation for, manufacture for, sale to, transfer to, or possession by the United States or a department or agency of the United States or a State or a department, agency, or political subdivision of a State, or a sale or transfer to or possession by a qualified law enforcement officer employed by the United States or a department or agency of the United States or a State or a department, agency, or political subdivision of a State, for purposes of law enforcement (whether on or off duty), or a sale or transfer to or possession by a campus law enforcement officer for purposes of law enforcement (whether on or off duty); or

"(ii) the importation for, or sale or transfer to a licensee under title I of the Atomic Energy Act of 1954 for purposes of establishing and maintaining an on-site physical protection system and security organization required by Federal law, or possession by an employee or contractor of such licensee on-site for such purposes or off-site for purposes of licensee-authorized training or transportation of nuclear materials.

"(B) DEFINITION.—For purposes of subparagraph (A), the term 'campus law enforcement officer' means an individual who is—

"(i) employed by a private institution of higher education that is eligible for funding under title IV of the Higher Education Act of 1965 (20 U.S.C. 1070 et seq.);

"(ii) responsible for the prevention or investigation of crime involving injury to persons or property, including apprehension or detention of persons for such crimes;

"(iii) authorized by Federal, State, or local law to carry a firearm, execute search warrants, and make arrests; and

"(iv) recognized, commissioned, or certified by a government entity as a law enforcement officer.

"(e) Prohibition Of Straw Purchasing.—It shall be unlawful for any person to willfully use a valid Federal or State firearm license to purchase a firearm or ammunition on behalf of another individual, regardless of whether the other individual has a valid Federal or State firearm license.

"(f) Penalties.—Any person who violates subsection (a) or (e) shall be imprisoned not more than 2 years, fined in accordance with this title, or both.

"(g) Database.—The Attorney General shall establish an electronic database, which shall be accessible by Federal, State, local, and Tribal law enforcement agencies and licensed dealers, through which a licensed dealer may verify the validity of a Federal firearm owner's license issued under this section.

"(h) Revocation Of Licenses.—

"(1) IN GENERAL.—The Attorney General shall revoke the Federal firearm owner's license issued to an individual under this section upon the occurrence of any event that would have disqualified the individual from being issued or renewed a Federal firearm owner's license under this section or for a violation of a restriction provided under this section.

"(2) REQUIRED NOTICE.—Upon revocation of a Federal firearm owner's license under paragraph (1), the Attorney General shall provide written notice of such revocation to the individual to whom the license was issued.

"(3) APPEAL OF REVOCATION.—

"(A) IN GENERAL.—An individual who has the Federal firearm owner's license of the individual revoked under this subsection may appeal the revocation determination to the Director of the Bureau of Alcohol, Tobacco, Firearms and Explosives.

"(B) REQUIREMENT.—Not later than 14 days after the date on which an individual appeals a revocation determination under subparagraph (A), the Director of the Bureau of Alcohol, Tobacco, Firearms and Explosives shall conduct a hearing on the appeal.

"(C) NOTICE OF DETERMINATION.—The Director of the Bureau of Alcohol, Tobacco, Firearms and Explosives shall provide written notice of the determination made after a hearing under subparagraph (B) regarding the appealed revocation to the individual.

"(D) APPEAL.—If the Director of the Bureau of Alcohol, Tobacco, Firearms and Explosives determines after a hearing under this paragraph to uphold the revocation, the determination may be appealed to an appropriate district court of the United States.

"(i) Authorization Of Appropriations.—There are authorized to be appropriated to the Attorney General such sums as are necessary to carry out this section.".

(b) Clerical Amendment.—The table of sections for such chapter is amended by adding at the end the following:

"932. License to own firearms and ammunition.".

(c) Effective Date.—The amendments made by subsections (a) and (b) shall take effect on the date that is 2 years after the date of enactment of this Act.

(d) Regulations.—

(1) IN GENERAL.—Not later than 1 year after the date of enactment of this Act, the Attorney General shall promulgate regulations to carry out section 932 of title 18, United States Code, as added by subsection (a), including a regulation requiring that any firearm manufactured after the effective date described in subsection (c) of this section be legibly and conspicuously engraved or cast with the date on which the firearm was manufactured.

(2) REQUIREMENT.—The Attorney General shall conduct, not less frequently than annually, a background investigation of each individual to whom a Federal firearm owner's license is issued under this section to ensure that the individual is not prohibited from possessing a firearm under subsection (g) or (n) of section 922 or under State law.

(e) Annual Report.—Not later than 1 year after the date of enactment of this Act, and each year thereafter, the Attorney General shall submit a report to Congress on the implementation of section 932 of title 18, United States Code, as added by subsection (a), and recommendations, if any, for improvements of the system required to be established under such section 932.

SEC. 102. STATE FIREARMS LICENSING.

(a) In General.—Title I of the Omnibus Crime Control and Safe Streets Act of 1968 (34 U.S.C. 10101 et seq.) is amended by adding at the end the following:
"PART OO—FIREARMS LICENSING
"SEC. 3051. DEFINITIONS.

"(a) In General.—In this part—

"(1) the term 'covered license' means a—

"(A) firearms license; or

"(B) firearms dealer license;

"(2) the term 'extreme risk protection order'—

"(A) means a written order, issued by a State court or signed by a magistrate that, for a period not to exceed a time frame established by the State—

"(i) prohibits the individual named in the order from having under the custody or control of the individual, purchasing, possessing, or receiving a firearm or ammunition; and

"(ii) requires that any firearm or ammunition under the custody or control of the individual be removed; and

"(B) does not include a domestic violence protection order, as defined in section 2266 of title 18, United States Code;

"(3) the term 'prohibited individual' means an individual who is categorically ineligible to receive a covered license;

"(4) the term 'suitable' means that an individual does not create a risk to public safety; and

"(5) the term 'thorough background check' means a Federal and State background check, which may include a fingerprint-based background check.

"(b) Prohibited Individuals.—For purposes of this part, a State—

"(1) shall establish standards for categorizing an individual as a prohibited individual for purposes of receiving a covered license; and

"(2) in establishing standards with respect to a covered license under paragraph (1), shall take into consideration whether limitations may be warranted based on—

"(A) criminal history;

"(B) whether an individual has been—

"(i) deemed a danger to himself or herself or other individuals by a court or authorized administrative body; or

"(ii) committed to a hospital or institution as a danger to himself or herself or other individuals;

"(C) age;

"(D) legal residency;

"(E) military dishonorable discharges;

"(F) whether an individual is subject to a permanent or temporary protection order or has ever been convicted of a misdemeanor crime of domestic violence;

"(G) outstanding arrest warrants;

"(H) status as a fugitive;

"(I) renunciation of United States citizenship; and

"(J) other factors relevant to the suitability of a license holder.

"SEC. 3052. GRANTS AND CONDITIONS.

"(a) Grants Authorized.—The Assistant Attorney General may make grants to States to implement or maintain firearms and firearms dealer licensing requirements.

"(b) Duration Of Grants.—A grant under subsection (a) shall be for a period of 3 fiscal years.

"(c) Use Of Funds For Firearms And Firearms Dealer Licensing.—

"(1) ACTIVITIES.—Amounts received under a grant under subsection (a) shall be used for the implementation or maintenance of firearms and firearms dealer licensing requirements, which shall incorporate and implement the elements described in paragraph (2).

"(2) ELEMENTS.—The elements described in this paragraph are those providing that—

"(A) an individual shall have a firearms license—

"(i) at the time of the purchase, rental, or lease of a firearm or purchase of ammunition; and

"(ii) during the entire period of ownership or possession of a firearm or ammunition;

"(B) (i) an individual who (including the owner or operator of a business that) sells, rents, or leases a minimum number of firearms, or sells ammunition, during a calendar year shall obtain a firearms dealer license; and

"(ii) the State shall establish the minimum number of firearms for purposes of clause (i), which may not be higher than 10 per calendar year;

"(C) the chief of police or the board or officer having control of the police department of a local government, or a designee within the same department, shall function as the licensing authority;

"(D) for an application for issuance or renewal of a firearms license, the licensing authority shall—

"(i) conduct a thorough background check, which may include—

"(I) conducting an interview with the applicant;

"(II) requiring the submission of letters of reference stating that the applicant is of sound mind and character; and

"(III) any other requirements the State determines relevant; and

"(ii) make a determination of suitability;

"(E) a first-time firearms license applicant shall complete safety training;

"(F) for an application for issuance or renewal of a firearms dealer license, the licensing authority shall conduct an investigation into the criminal history of the applicant, which may include—

"(i) an interview with the applicant;

"(ii) a thorough background check; and

"(iii) any other requirements the State determines relevant;

"(G) the State shall establish appropriate application processes for covered licenses consistent with Federal, State, and local law;

"(H) the State shall establish standards and processes by which licensing authorities can revoke, suspend, or deny the issuance or renewal of a covered license;

"(I) the State shall ensure that a revocation, suspension, or denial cannot be based on race, color, ethnicity, religion, sex, sexual orientation, or gender identity;

"(J) the State shall establish judicial review processes by which any applicant for or holder of a covered license may, within a reasonable time period, petition to obtain judicial review of a revocation, suspension, or denial of the issuance or renewal of a covered license;

"(K) the State shall establish—

"(i) standards and a process under which a family member of an individual who the family member fears is a danger to himself, herself, or others may petition for an extreme risk protection order; and

"(ii) standards for the termination or extension of an order described in clause (i);

"(L) the State shall establish processes under which—

"(i) an individual whose covered license is revoked or suspended, or whose application for issuance or renewal of a covered license is denied, shall surrender or transfer all firearms and ammunition that are or would have been covered by the license; and

"(ii) an individual who is subject to an extreme risk protection order or a domestic protection order, as defined in section 2266 of title 18, United States Code, shall surrender or transfer all firearms and ammunition in the possession of the individual;

"(M) the State shall establish requirements with which a firearms dealer licensee must comply, which—

"(i) shall include requirements relating to—

"(I) the location at which the licensee conducts firearm or ammunition transactions;

"(II) the manner in which the licensee records firearm or ammunition transactions;

"(III) background checks for employees of the licensee; and

"(IV) any other matter that the State determines appropriate; and

"(ii) may include requirements that a licensee—

"(I) maintain a permanent place of business—

"(aa) that is not a residence; and

"(bb) at which the licensee conducts all firearms or ammunition transactions;

"(II) submit to mandatory record and inventory inspections by a licensing authority;

"(III) maintain a sales record book at the permanent place of business described in subclause (I) in accordance with standards established by the State;

"(IV) conduct a pre-employment background check on each potential employee to determine the suitability of any potential employee who may have direct and unmonitored contact with a firearm or ammunition; and

"(V) take any other action that the State determines appropriate;

"(N) the State shall promulgate rules and regulations to ensure the prompt collection, exchange, dissemination, and distribution of information pertaining to the issuance, renewal, expiration, suspension, or revocation of a covered license;

"(O) the State shall establish standards that are consistent with Federal and State law—

"(i) governing the transfer of a firearm or ammunition; and

"(ii) for identifying a prohibited individual, in accordance with section 3051(b);

"(P) the State shall promulgate rules and regulations that require a dealer or private seller of firearms or ammunition to verify the validity of a firearms license before the sale, rental, or lease of any firearm or the sale of any ammunition;

"(Q) a dealer or private seller of firearms or ammunition shall report all sales, rentals, and leases of firearms, and sales of ammunition, to State authorities;

"(R) a dealer of firearms or ammunition shall notify the licensing authority when presented with an invalid or expired firearms license;

"(S) any firearms licensee whose firearm or ammunition is lost or stolen shall report the loss or theft to the licensing authority and State authorities within a reasonable time frame and in a manner established by the State;

"(T) an individual holding a firearms license or firearms dealer license shall renew the license on a time frame established by the State;

"(U) an individual may not use the firearms license of the individual to purchase a firearm or ammunition for—

"(i) the unlawful use of the firearm or ammunition by another individual; or

"(ii) the resale or other transfer of the firearm or ammunition to an unlicensed individual; and

"(V) (i) it shall be unlawful to store or keep a firearm in any place unless the firearm is secured in a locked container or equipped with a tamper-resistant mechanical lock or other safety device, properly engaged so as to render the firearm inoperable by any individual other than the owner or other lawfully authorized user; and

"(ii) for purposes of clause (i), a firearm shall not be considered to be stored or kept if carried by or under the control of the owner or other lawfully authorized user.

"(3) SEPARATE AMMUNITION DEALER LICENSE PERMITTED.—A State that requires a license for dealing ammunition that is separate from a license for dealing firearms shall be deemed to have satisfied the requirements under paragraph (2) relating to a firearms dealer license, as that license relates to the dealing of ammunition, if the State imposes the same requirements for an ammunition dealer license as are mandated under paragraph (2) for a firearms dealer license, as that license relates to the dealing of ammunition.

"(d) Application.—To be eligible to receive a grant under subsection (a), a State shall submit to the Assistant Attorney General an application at such time, in such manner, and containing such information as the Assistant Attorney General may require, including a description of how the State will use the grant to implement or maintain firearms and firearms dealer licensing requirements that include the elements described in subsection (c)(2).

"(e) Annual Report.—Each State receiving a grant under this section shall submit to the Assistant Attorney General, for each fiscal year during which the State expends amounts received under the grant, a report, at such time and in such manner as the Assistant Attorney General may reasonably require, that contains—

"(1) a summary of the activities carried out using amounts made available under the grant;

"(2) an assessment of whether the activities are achieving the elements described in subsection (c)

(2); and

"(3) such other information as the Assistant Attorney General may require.

"(f) Limitations On The Allocation Of Funds.—Not more than 2 percent of the amount made available to carry out this section in any fiscal year may be used by the Assistant Attorney General for salaries and administrative expenses.

"(g) Reallocation Of Appropriations.—A recipient of a grant under subsection (a) shall return to the Assistant Attorney General any amounts received under the grant that are not expended for a purpose described in this section.".

(b) Authorization Of Appropriations.—Section 1001(a) of title I of the Omnibus Crime Control and Safe Streets Act of 1968 (34 U.S.C. 10261(a)) is amended by adding at the end the following:
"(29) There are authorized to be appropriated such sums as may be necessary to carry out part OO.".

TITLE II—BACKGROUND CHECK REFORM

SEC. 201. UNIVERSAL BACKGROUND CHECKS.

(a) In General.—Section 922 of title 18, United States Code, as amended by this Act, is amended—

(1) by repealing subsection (s);

(2) by redesignating subsection (t) as subsection (s);

(3) in subsection (s), as redesignated—

(A) in paragraph (1)—

(i) by redesignating subparagraphs (A), (B), and (C) as subparagraphs (B), (C), and (D), respectively; and

(ii) by inserting before subparagraph (B), as so re-designated, the following:
"(A) beginning on the date that the database is established under section 932(g), before completion of the transfer, the licensee verifies, using such database, that the purchaser has a valid—

"(i) Federal firearm owner's license issued under section 932; or

"(ii) qualifying State firearm license, as described in section 932(d)(2), for the State in which the transfer will occur;"; and

(B) in paragraph (3)—

(i) by striking subparagraph (A);

(ii) by redesignating subparagraphs (B) and (C) as subparagraphs (A) and (B), respectively; and

(iii) in subparagraph (B)(ii), as so redesignated, by striking "(as defined in subsection (s)(8))"; and

(4) by inserting after subsection (s), as so redesignated, the following:

"(t) (1) (A) Beginning on the date that is 180 days after the date of enactment of the Gun Violence Prevention and Community Safety Act of 2020, it shall be unlawful for any person who is not a licensed importer, licensed manufacturer, or licensed dealer to transfer a firearm to any other person who is not so licensed, unless a licensed importer, licensed manufacturer, or licensed dealer has first taken possession of the firearm for the purpose of complying with subsection (s).

"(B) Upon taking possession of a firearm under subparagraph (A), a licensee shall comply with all requirements of this chapter as if the licensee were transferring the firearm from the inventory of the licensee to the unlicensed transferee.

"(C) If a transfer of a firearm described in subparagraph (A) will not be completed for any reason after a licensee takes possession of the firearm (including because the transfer of the firearm to, or receipt of the firearm by, the transferee would violate this chapter), the return of the firearm to the transferor by the licensee shall not constitute the transfer of a firearm for purposes of this chapter.

"(2) Paragraph (1) shall not apply to—

"(A) a law enforcement agency or any law enforcement officer, armed private security professional, or member of the armed forces, to the extent the officer, professional, or member is acting within the course and scope of employment and official duties;

"(B) a transfer that is a loan or bona fide gift between spouses, between domestic partners, between parents and their children, between siblings, between aunts or uncles and their nieces or nephews, or between grandparents and their grandchildren, if the transferor has no reason to believe that the transferee—

"(i) will use or intends to use the firearm in a crime or is prohibited from possessing firearms under Federal, State, Tribal, or local law;

"(ii) has committed domestic violence (as defined in section 40002 of the Violence Against Women Act of 1994 (34 U.S.C. 12291) or by the jurisdiction in which the transfer is occurring or in which the transferee resides); or "(iii) is subject to a protection order (as defined in section 2266);

"(C) a transfer to an executor, administrator, trustee, or personal representative of an estate or a trust that occurs by operation of law upon the death of another person;

"(D) a temporary transfer that is necessary to prevent imminent death or great bodily harm, if the possession by the transferee lasts only as long as immediately necessary to prevent the imminent death or great bodily harm;

"(E) a transfer that is approved by the Attorney General under section 5812 of the Internal Revenue Code of 1986; or

"(F) a temporary transfer if the transferor has no reason to believe that the transferee will use or intends to use the firearm in a crime or is prohibited from possessing firearms under State, Federal, Tribal, or local law, and no reason to believe that the transferee has committed domestic violence (as defined in section 40002 of the Violence Against Women Act of 1994 (34 U.S.C. 12291) or by the jurisdiction in which the transfer is occurring or in which the transferee resides) or is subject to a protection order (as defined in section 2266), and the transfer takes place and the transferee's possession of the firearm is exclusively—

"(i) at a shooting range or in a shooting gallery or other area designated for the purpose of target shooting;

"(ii) while reasonably necessary for the purposes of hunting, trapping, or fishing, if the transferor—

"(I) has no reason to believe that the transferee intends to use the firearm in a place where it is illegal; and

"(II) has reason to believe that the transferee will comply with all licensing and permit requirements for such hunting, trapping, or fishing; or

"(iii) while in the presence of the transferor.".

(b) Technical And Conforming Amendments.—

(1) SECTION 922.—Section 922(y)(2) of title 18, United States Code, is amended, in the matter preceding subparagraph (A), by striking ", (g)(5)(B), and (s)(3)(B)(v)(II)" and inserting "and (g)(5)(B)".

(2) SECTION 925A.—Section 925A of title 18, United States Code, is amended, in the matter preceding paragraph (1), by striking "subsection (s) or

(t) of section 922" and inserting "section 922(s)".

SEC. 202. COMPLETION OF BACKGROUND CHECKS; 7-DAY WAITING PERIOD.

Section 922(s)(1)(C) of title 18, United States Code, as amended by section 201 of this Act, is amended—

(1) in clause (i), by striking "; or" and inserting "; and"; and

(2) in clause (ii)—

(A) by striking "3 business" and inserting "not less than 7 business"; and

(B) by striking ", and the" and all that follows through "this section".

SEC. 203. REPORTING OF BACKGROUND CHECK DENIALS.

(a) In General.—Chapter 44 of title 18, United States Code, is amended by inserting after section 925A the following:

"§ 925B. Reporting of background check denials to State authorities

"(a) In General.—If the national instant criminal background check system established under section 103 of the Brady Handgun Violence Prevention Act (34 U.S.C. 40901) (commonly referred to as 'NICS') provides a notice pursuant to section 922(s) of this title that the receipt of a firearm by a person would violate subsection (g) or (n) of section 922 of this title or State law, the Attorney General shall, in accordance with subsection (b) of this section—

"(1) report to the law enforcement authorities of the State where the person sought to acquire the firearm and, if different, the law enforcement authorities of the State of residence of the person—

"(A) that the notice was provided;

"(B) the specific provision of law that would have been violated;

"(C) the date and time the notice was provided;

"(D) the location where the firearm was sought to be acquired; and

"(E) the identity of the person; and

"(2) where practicable, report the incident to local law enforcement authorities and State and local prosecutors in the jurisdiction where the firearm was sought and in the jurisdiction where the person resides.

"(b) Requirements For Report.—A report is made

in accordance with this section if the report is made within 24 hours after the provision of the notice described in subsection (a), except that the making of the report may be delayed for so long as is necessary to avoid compromising an ongoing investigation.

"(c) Amendment Of Report.—If a report is made in accordance with this section and, after such report is made, the Federal Bureau of Investigation or the Bureau of Alcohol, Tobacco, Firearms and Explosives determines that the receipt of a firearm by a person for whom the report was made would not violate subsection (g) or (n) of section 922 of this title or State law, the Attorney General shall, in accordance with subsection (b), notify any law enforcement authority and any prosecutor to whom the report was made of that determination.

"(d) Rule Of Construction.—Nothing in subsection (a) shall be construed to require a report with respect to a person to be made to the same State authorities that originally issued the notice with respect to the person.

"§ 925C. Annual report to Congress

"Not later than 1 year after the date of enactment of this section, and annually thereafter, the Attorney General shall submit to Congress a report detailing the following, broken down by Federal judicial district:

"(1) With respect to each category of persons prohibited by subsection (g) or (n) of section 922 of this title or State law from receiving or possessing a firearm who are so denied a firearm—

"(A) the number of denials;

"(B) the number of denials referred to the Bureau of Alcohol, Tobacco, Firearms and Explosives;

"(C) the number of denials for which the Bureau of Alcohol, Tobacco, Firearms and Explosives determines that the person denied was not prohibited by subsection (g) or (n) of section 922 of this title or State law from receiving or possessing a firearm;

"(D) the number of denials overturned through the national instant criminal background check system appeals process and the reasons for overturning the denials;

"(E) the number of denials with respect to which an investigation was opened by a field division of the Bureau of Alcohol, Tobacco, Firearms and Explosives;

"(F) the number of persons charged with a Federal criminal offense in connection with a denial; and

"(G) the number of convictions obtained by Federal

authorities in connection with a denial.

"(2) The number of background check notices reported to State authorities pursuant to section 925B (including the number of the notices that would have been so reported but for section 925B(c)).".

(b) Clerical Amendment.—The table of sections for chapter 44 of title 18, United States Code, is amended by inserting after the item relating to section 925A the following:
"925B. Reporting of background check denials to State authorities.
"925C. Annual report to Congress.".

TITLE III—FIREARM POSSESSION

SEC. 301. PROTECTING VICTIMS OF DOMESTIC VIOLENCE.

(a) Definition.—Section 921(a) of title 18, United States Code, is amended—

(1) by striking paragraph (32) and inserting the following:
"(32) The term 'intimate partner' means, with respect to a person, the spouse of the person, a former spouse of the person, an individual who cohabitates or has cohabited with the person, a dating partner or former dating partner (as defined in section 2266) of the person, and any other person similarly situated to a spouse who is protected by the do-

mestic or family violence laws of the jurisdiction in which the injury occurred or where the victim resides.";

(2) in paragraph (33)(A)—

(A) in the matter preceding clause (i), by striking "Except as provided in subparagraph (C), the term" and inserting "The term";

(B) in clause (i), by inserting "municipal," after "State,"; and

(C) in clause (ii), by inserting "dating partner (as defined in section 2266)," after "spouse," each place the term appears; and

(3) by adding at the end the following:
"(36) (A) The term 'misdemeanor crime of stalking' means an offense that—

"(i) is a misdemeanor crime of stalking under Federal, State, Tribal, or municipal law; and

"(ii) is a course of harassment, intimidation, or surveillance of another person that—

"(I) places that person in reasonable fear of material harm to the health or safety of—

"(aa) that person;

"(bb) an immediate family member (as defined in section 115) of that person;

"(cc) a household member of that person; or

"(dd) a spouse or intimate partner of that person; or

"(II) causes, attempts to cause, or would reasonably be expected to cause emotional distress to a person described in item (aa), (bb), (cc), or (dd) of subclause (I).

"(B) A person shall not be considered to have been convicted of such an offense for purposes of this chapter, unless—

"(i) the person was represented by counsel in the case, or knowingly and intelligently waived the right to counsel in the case; and

"(ii) in the case of a prosecution for an offense described in this paragraph for which a person was entitled to a jury trial in the jurisdiction in which the case was tried, either—

"(I) the case was tried by a jury; or

"(II) the person knowingly and intelligently waived

the right to have the case tried by a jury, by guilty plea or otherwise.

"(C) A person shall not be considered to have been convicted of such an offense for purposes of this chapter if the conviction has been expunged or set aside, or is an offense for which the person has been pardoned or has had civil rights restored (if the law of the applicable jurisdiction provides for the loss of civil rights under such an offense) unless the pardon, expungement, or restoration of civil rights expressly provides that the person may not ship, transport, possess, or receive firearms.".

(b) Addition Of Stalking And Those Subject To Court Order.—Section 922 of title 18, United States Code, is amended—

(1) in subsection (d)—

(A) in paragraph (8)—

(i) in the matter preceding clause (i), by striking "that restrains such person" and all that follows and inserting "described in subsection (g)(8);"; and

(ii) by striking subparagraphs (A) and (B);

(B) in paragraph (9), by striking the period at the end and inserting a semicolon; and

(C) by inserting after paragraph (9) the following: "(10) has been convicted in any court of a misdemeanor crime of stalking; or"; and

(2) in subsection (g)—

(A) by amending paragraph (8) to read as follows: "(8) who is subject to a court order—

"(A) that was issued—

"(i) after a hearing of which such person received actual notice, and at which such person had an opportunity to participate; or

"(ii) in the case of an ex parte order, relative to which notice and opportunity to be heard are provided—

"(I) within the time required by State, tribal, or territorial law; and

"(II) in any event within a reasonable time after the order is issued, sufficient to protect the due process rights of the person;

"(B) that restrains such person from—

"(i) harassing, stalking, or threatening an intimate

partner of such person or child of such intimate partner or person, or engaging in other conduct that would place an intimate partner in reasonable fear of bodily injury to the partner or child; or

"(ii) intimidating or dissuading a witness from testifying in court; and

"(C) that—

"(i) includes a finding that such person represents a credible threat to the physical safety of such individual described in subparagraph (B); or

"(ii) by its terms explicitly prohibits the use, attempted use, or threatened use of physical force against such individual described in subparagraph (B) that would reasonably be expected to cause bodily injury;";

(B) in paragraph (9), by striking the comma at the end and inserting a semicolon; and

(C) by inserting after paragraph (9) the following:
"(10) has been convicted in any court of a misdemeanor crime of stalking; or".

SEC. 302. FUGITIVES FROM JUSTICE.

Chapter 44 of title 18, United States Code, is amended—

(1) in section 921(a)(15) of title 18, United States Code, is amended—

(A) by striking the period at the end and inserting "; or"; and

(B) by adding at the end the following:
"(B) is subject to an outstanding arrest warrant issued by any court."; and

(2) in section 922(g)(2) of title 18, United States Code, is amended by inserting "knows that he or she" after "who".

SEC. 303. MINIMUM AGE FOR PURCHASING FIREARMS AND AMMUNITION.

(a) In General.—Chapter 44 of title 18, United States Code, is amended—

(1) in section 922—

(A) in subsection (a)—

(i) in paragraph (2)(A), by striking "(b)(3)" and inserting "(b)(2)";

(ii) in paragraph (3), by striking "(b)(3)" and inserting "(b)(2)";

(iii) in paragraph (9), by striking the period at the end and inserting "; and"; and

(iv) by adding at the end the following:
"(10) for any person to transfer, sell, trade, give, transport, or deliver any firearm or ammunition to any person who the transferor knows or has reasonable cause to believe is less than 21 years of age, except that this paragraph shall not apply to—

"(A) a temporary transfer of a firearm or ammunition to a person who is less than 21 years of age or to the possession or use of a firearm or ammunition by a person who is less than 21 years of age if the firearm or ammunition is possessed and used by the person—

"(i) in the course of employment, in the course of ranching or farming related to activities at the residence of the person (or on property used for ranching or farming at which the person, with the permission of the property owner or lessee, is performing activities related to the operation of the farm or ranch), target practice, hunting, or a course of instruction in the safe and lawful use of a firearm;

"(ii) with the prior written consent of the person's parent or guardian who is not prohibited by Federal, State, or local law from possessing a firearm, except—

"(I) during transportation by the person of an un-loaded firearm in a locked container directly from the place of transfer to a place at which an activity described in clause (i) is to take place and trans-portation by the person of that firearm, unloaded and in a locked container, directly from the place at which such an activity took place to the transferor; or

"(II) with respect to ranching or farming activities as described in clause (i), a person who is less than 21 years of age may possess and use a firearm or ammunition with the prior written approval of the person's parent or legal guardian and at the direc-tion of an adult who is not prohibited by Federal, State or local law from possessing a firearm;

"(iii) the person has the prior written consent in the person's possession at all times when a firearm or ammunition is in the possession of the person; and

"(iv) in accordance with State and local law;

"(B) a person who is less than 21 years of age who is a member of the Armed Forces of the United States or the National Guard who possesses or is armed with a firearm or ammunition in the line of duty;

"(C) a transfer by inheritance of title (but not possession) of a firearm or ammunition to a person who is less than 21 years of age; or

"(D) the possession of a firearm or ammunition by a person who is less than 21 years of age for the purpose described in subsection (x)(3)(D).";

(B) in subsection (b)—

(i) by striking paragraph (1);

(ii) by redesignating paragraphs (2), (3), (4), and (5) as paragraphs (1), (2), (3), and (4), respectively; and

(iii) in the undesignated matter following paragraph (4), as so redesignated—

(I) in the first sentence, by striking "Paragraphs (1), (2), (3), and (4)" and inserting "Subsection (a)(10) and paragraphs (1), (2), and (3)"; and

(II) in the second sentence, by striking "Paragraph (4)" and inserting "Paragraph (3)"; and

(C) in subsection (c)(1), by striking ", in the case of any firearm other than a shotgun or a rifle, I am twenty-one years or more of age, or that, in the case of a shotgun or a rifle, I am eighteen years or more of age" and inserting "I am 21 years or more of age"; and

(2) in section 924—

(A) in subsection (a)(6), by striking "handgun" each place the term appears and inserting "firearm"; and

(B) in subsection (d)(3)(C), by striking "922(b)(3)" each place the term appears and inserting "922(b)(2)".

(b) Technical And Conforming Amendments.—

(1) Section 4182(d) of the Internal Revenue Code of 1986 is amended by striking "922(b)(5)" and inserting "922(b)(4)".

(2) Section 161A(b) of the Atomic Energy Act of 1954 (42 U.S.C. 2201a(b)) is amended, in the matter preceding paragraph (1), by striking "(b)(2), (b)(4)" and inserting "(b)(1), (b)(3)".

SEC. 304. SECURE GUN STORAGE BY OWNERS.

Section 922(z) of title 18, United States Code, is amended by adding at the end the following:
"(4) SECURE GUN STORAGE BY OWNERS.—

"(A) OFFENSE.—

"(i) IN GENERAL.—Except as provided in clause

(ii), it shall be unlawful for a person to store or keep any firearm that has moved in, or that has otherwise affected, interstate or foreign commerce on the premises of a residence under the control of the person if the person knows, or reasonably should know, that—

"(I) a minor is likely to gain access to the firearm without the permission of the parent or guardian of the minor; or

"(II) a resident of the residence is ineligible to possess a firearm under Federal, State, or local law.

"(ii) EXCEPTION.—Clause (i) shall not apply to a person if the person—

"(I) keeps the firearm—

"(aa) secure using a secure gun storage or safety device; or

"(bb) in a location which a reasonable person would believe to be secure; or

"(II) carries the firearm on his or her person or within such close proximity thereto that the person can readily retrieve and use the firearm as if the person carried the firearm on his or her person.

"(B) PENALTY.—

"(i) IN GENERAL.—Any person who violates subparagraph (A) shall be subject to a $500 civil penalty per violation.

"(ii) ENHANCED PENALTY.—If a person violates subparagraph (A) and a minor or a resident who is ineligible to possess a firearm under Federal, State, or local law obtains the firearm, the person shall be fined under this title, imprisoned for not more than 5 years, or both.

"(iii) FORFEITURE OF IMPROPERLY STORED FIREARM.—Any firearm stored in violation of subparagraph (A) shall be subject to seizure and forfeiture in accordance with the procedures described in section 924(d).

"(C) MINOR DEFINED.—In this paragraph, the term 'minor' means an individual who is less than 18 years of age.".

SEC. 305. SECURE GUN STORAGE OR SAFETY DEVICE FOR ALL FIREARMS.

Section 922(z) of title 18, United States Code, is amended by striking "handgun" each place it appears and inserting "firearm".

SEC. 306. CONSUMER PRODUCT SAFETY

STANDARDS FOR GUN LOCKS AND GUN SAFES.

(a) In General.—The Consumer Product Safety Act (15 U.S.C. 2051 et seq.) is amended by adding at the end the following:

"SEC. 43. CONSUMER PRODUCT SAFETY STANDARDS FOR FIREARM LOCKS AND FIREARM SAFES.

"(a) Establishment Of Standards.—

"(1) RULEMAKING REQUIRED.—

"(A) RULEMAKING PROCEEDING.—Notwithstanding section 3(a)(5)(E), the Commission shall initiate a rulemaking proceeding under section 553 of title 5, United States Code, within 90 days after the date of the enactment of this section to establish—

"(i) a consumer product safety standard for firearm locks; and

"(ii) a consumer product safety standard for firearm safes.

"(B) FINAL RULE.—Notwithstanding any other provision of law, including chapter 5 of title 5, United States Code, the Commission shall promulgate final consumer product safety standards under this paragraph within 12 months after the date on which the Commission initiates the rulemaking proceeding under subparagraph (A).

"(C) EFFECTIVE DATE.—Each final consumer product safety standard promulgated under this paragraph shall take effect 6 months after the date on which such standard is promulgated.

"(2) REQUIREMENTS FOR FIREARM LOCK STANDARD.—The standard for firearm locks promulgated under paragraph (1) shall require firearm locks that—

"(A) are sufficiently difficult for an unauthorized user to de-activate or remove; and

"(B) prevent the discharge of the firearm unless the firearm lock has been de-activated or removed.

"(3) REQUIREMENTS FOR FIREARM SAFE STANDARD.—The standard for firearm safes promulgated under paragraph (1) shall require firearm safes that reliably secure firearms from unauthorized users, and include reliable security features, quality, and construction to reliably prevent unauthorized users from gaining access to a firearm by damaging or physically manipulating the safe.

"(b) Certain Provisions Not To Apply.—

"(1) PROVISIONS OF THIS ACT.—Sections 7 and 9 of this Act do not apply to the rulemaking proceeding under paragraph (1) of subsection (a).

"(2) CHAPTER 5 OF TITLE 5.—Except for section 553, chapter 5 of title 5, United States Code, does not apply to this section.

"(3) CHAPTER 6 OF TITLE 5.—Chapter 6 of title 5, United States Code, does not apply to this section.

"(4) NATIONAL ENVIRONMENTAL POLICY ACT.—The National Environmental Policy Act of 1969 (42 U.S.C. 4321 et seq.) does not apply to this section.

"(c) No Effect On State Law.—Notwithstanding section 26 of this Act, this section does not annul, alter, impair, affect, or exempt any person subject to a consumer product safety standard promulgated under subsection (a)(1) from complying with any provision of the law of any State or any political subdivision thereof, except to the extent that such provision is inconsistent with any such standard, and then only to the extent of the inconsistency. A provision of the law of a State or a political subdivision thereof is not inconsistent with a consumer product safety standard promulgated under subsection (a)(1) if such provision affords greater protection to individuals with respect to firearms than is afforded by such standard.

"(d) Enforcement.—Notwithstanding subsection (b)(1), the consumer product safety standards promulgated by the Commission under subsection (a)(1) shall be enforced under this Act as if such standards were consumer product safety standards described in section 7(a).

"(e) Definitions.—In this section:

"(1) FIREARM.—The term 'firearm' has the meaning given the term in section 921(a) of title 18, United States Code.

"(2) FIREARM LOCK.—The term 'firearm lock' means any disabling or locking device that is not built into the firearm at the time of manufacture and that is designed to prevent the firearm from being discharged unless the device has been deactivated or removed.

"(3) FIREARM SAFE.—The term 'firearm safe' means a container that is advertised to be used to store a firearm and that is designed to be unlocked only by means of a key, a combination, or other similar means.".

(b) Conforming Amendment.—Section 1 of the Consumer Product Safety Act is amended by adding at the end of the table of contents the following: "Sec. 43. Consumer product safety standards for firearm locks and firearm safes.".
(c) Authorization Of Appropriations.—There are authorized to be appropriated to the Consumer Product Safety Commission $2,000,000 to carry out the provisions of section 43 of the Consumer Product Safety Act, as added by subsection (a), such sums to remain available until expended.

SEC. 307. GUN-FREE SCHOOL ZONES.

(a) Extension Of Gun-Free School Zones Act To Colleges And Universities.—Section 921(a) of title 18, United States Code, is amended—

(1) in paragraph (25), by striking "public, parochial or private" each place that term appears; and

(2) in paragraph (26)—

(A) by striking "means a school" and inserting the following: "means—

"(A) a public, parochial, or private school"; and

(B) by striking the period at the end and inserting

the following: "; and

"(B) an institution of higher education, as defined in section 102 of the Higher Education Act of 1965 (20 U.S.C. 1002).".

(b) Elimination Of Exception For Licensed Individuals.—Section 922(q)(2)(B) of title 18, United States Code, is amended—

(1) by striking clause (ii); and

(2) by redesignating clauses (iii) through (vii) as clauses (ii) through (vi), respectively.

TITLE IV—EXTREME RISK PROTECTION ORDERS

SEC. 401. EXTREME RISK PROTECTION ORDER GRANT PROGRAM.

(a) Definitions.—In this section:

(1) ELIGIBLE ENTITY.—The term "eligible entity" means—

(A) a State or Indian Tribe—

(i) that enacts legislation described in subsection (c);

(ii) with respect to which the Attorney General determines that the legislation described in subsection (c) complies with the requirements of this section; and

(iii) that certifies to the Attorney General that the State or Indian Tribe shall—

(I) use the grant for the purposes described in this section; and

(II) allocate not less than 25 percent of the amount received under a grant under this section for training for law enforcement; or

(B) a unit of local government or other public or private entity that—

(i) is located in a State or in the territory under the jurisdiction of an Indian Tribe that meets the requirements of subparagraph (A); and

(ii) certifies to the Attorney General that the unit of local government or entity shall—

(I) use the grant for the purposes described in this section; and

(II) allocate not less than 25 percent of the amount received under a grant under this section for training for law enforcement.

(2) EXTREME RISK PROTECTION ORDER.—

(A) IN GENERAL.—The term "extreme risk protection order" means a written order or warrant, issued by a State, Tribal, or local court or signed by a magistrate (or other comparable judicial officer), the primary purpose of which is to reduce the risk of firearm-related death or injury by doing 1 or more of the following:

(i) Prohibiting a named individual from having under the custody or control of the individual, owning, purchasing, possessing, or receiving a firearm.

(ii) Having a firearm removed or requiring the surrender of firearms from a named individual.

(B) EXCLUSION.—The term "extreme risk protection order" does not include a domestic violence protection order, as defined in section 2266 of title 18, United States Code.

(3) FIREARM.—The term "firearm" has the meaning given the term in section 921 of title 18, United States Code.

(4) INDIAN TRIBE.—The term "Indian Tribe" has the meaning given the term "Indian tribe" in sec-

tion 1709 of the Omnibus Crime Control and Safe Streets Act of 1968 (34 U.S.C. 10389).

(5) LAW ENFORCEMENT OFFICER.—The term "law enforcement officer" means a public servant authorized by State, local, or tribal law or by a State, local, or tribal government agency to—

(A) engage in or supervise the prevention, detection, investigation, or prosecution of an offense; or

(B) supervise sentenced criminal offenders.

(6) PETITIONER.—The term "petitioner" means an individual authorized under State or tribal law to petition for an extreme risk protection order.

(7) STATE.—The term "State" means—

(A) any State;

(B) the District of Columbia;

(C) the Commonwealth of Puerto Rico; and

(D) any other territory or possession of the United States.

(8) UNIT OF LOCAL GOVERNMENT.—The term "unit of local government" has the meaning given

the term in section 901 of title I of the Omnibus Crime Control and Safe Streets Act of 1968 (34 U.S.C. 10251).

(b) Grant Program Established.—

(1) IN GENERAL.—The Director of the Office of Community Oriented Policing Services of the Department of Justice shall establish a program under which, from amounts made available to carry out this section, the Director may make grants to eligible entities to assist in carrying out the provisions of the legislation described in this section.

(2) USE OF FUNDS.—Funds awarded under this section may be used by an applicant to—

(A) enhance the capacity of law enforcement agencies and the courts of a State, unit of local government, or Indian Tribe by providing personnel, training, technical assistance, data collection, and other resources to carry out legislation described in this section;

(B) train judges, court personnel, and law enforcement officers to more accurately identify individuals whose access to firearms poses a danger of causing harm to themselves or others by increasing the risk of firearms suicide or interpersonal violence;

(C) develop and implement law enforcement and court protocols, forms, and orders so that law enforcement agencies and the courts may carry out the provisions of the legislation described in this section in a safe and effective manner, including through the removal and storage of firearms pursuant to extreme risk protection orders under the legislation; and

(D) raise public awareness and understanding of the legislation described in this section so that extreme risk protection orders may be issued in appropriate situations to reduce the risk of firearms-related death and injury.

(3) APPLICATION.—An eligible entity desiring a grant under this section shall submit to the Attorney General an application at such time, in such manner, and containing or accompanied by such information as the Attorney General may reasonably require.

(4) INCENTIVES.—For each of fiscal years 2020 through 2024, the Attorney General shall give affirmative preference in awarding any discretionary grant awarded by the Office of Community Oriented Policing Services to a State or Indian Tribe that has enacted legislation described in this section.

(5) AUTHORIZATION OF APPROPRIATIONS.—

There are authorized to be appropriated such sums as are necessary to carry out this section.

(c) Eligibility For Extreme Risk Protection Order Grant Program.—

(1) REQUIREMENTS.—Legislation described in this section is legislation that establishes requirements that are substantially similar to the following:

(A) APPLICATION FOR EXTREME RISK PROTECTION ORDER.—A petitioner, including a law enforcement officer, may submit an application to a State or tribal court, on a form designed by the court, State, or tribal agency, that—

(i) describes the facts and circumstances justifying that an extreme risk protection order be issued against the named individual; and

(ii) is signed by the applicant, under oath.

(B) NOTICE AND DUE PROCESS.—The individual named in an application for an extreme risk protection order described in subparagraph (A) shall be given written notice of the application and an opportunity to be heard on the matter in accordance with this section.

(C) ISSUANCE OF EXTREME RISK PROTEC-

TION ORDERS.—

(i) HEARING.—

(I) IN GENERAL.—Upon receipt of an application described in subparagraph (A) or request of an individual named in the application, the court shall order a hearing to be held within a reasonable time, no later than 30 days after the date on which the application or request is made.

(II) DETERMINATION.—If the court finds by a preponderance of the evidence or a higher evidentiary standard established by a State that the respondent poses a danger of causing harm to the respondent or others by having access to a firearm, the court may issue an extreme risk protection order.

(ii) DURATION OF EXTREME RISK PROTECTION ORDER.—An extreme risk protection order shall be in effect—

(I) until an order terminating or superseding the order is issued; or

(II) for a set period of time.

(D) EX PARTE EXTREME RISK PROTECTION ORDERS.—

(i) IN GENERAL.—Upon receipt of an application described in subparagraph (A), the court may issue an ex parte extreme risk protection order, if—

(I) the application for an extreme risk protection order alleges that the respondent poses a danger of causing harm to the respondent or others by having access to a firearm; and

(II) the court finds there is reasonable cause to believe, or makes a finding under such other, higher evidentiary standard as a State may establish, that the respondent poses a danger of causing harm to the respondent or others by having access to a firearm.

(ii) DURATION OF EX PARTE EXTREME RISK PROTECTION ORDER.—An ex parte extreme risk protection order shall remain in effect only until the hearing required under this section.

(E) STORAGE OF REMOVED FIREARMS.—

(i) IN GENERAL.—All firearms removed or surrendered pursuant to an extreme risk protection order shall be retained by a law enforcement officer or a law enforcement agency until the named individual regains eligibility to possess firearms.

(ii) AUTHORITY OF LAW ENFORCEMENT.—A

law enforcement agency may—

(I) contract with a manufacturer, dealer, or importer licensed under chapter 44 of title 18, United States Code, for the secure storage of firearms retained as described in clause (i); and

(II) transfer a firearm described in clause (i) upon proof that the named individual will no longer have access to the firearm.

(F) NOTIFICATION.—

(i) IN GENERAL.—A State or tribal court that issues an extreme risk protection order shall notify the Attorney General or the comparable State or tribal agency, as applicable, of the order as soon as practicable or within a designated period of time.

(ii) ELECTRONIC FORMAT.—A notice required under clause (i) shall be submitted in an electronic format, in a manner prescribed by the Attorney General or the comparable State or tribal agency.

(iii) UPDATE OF DATABASES.—As soon as is practicable or within a designated period of time after receiving a notification under clause (i), the Attorney General or the comparable State or tribal agency shall ensure the extreme risk protection order is reflected in the National Instant Criminal

Background Check System.

(G) CONFIDENTIALITY PROTECTIONS.—All personally identifiable information provided to the court, the Department of Justice, and comparable State or tribal agencies shall be kept confidential, as required by the laws of the relevant jurisdiction, except as necessary to carry out this Act.

(2) ADDITIONAL PROVISIONS.—Legislation described in this subsection may—

(A) provide procedures for the termination of an extreme risk protection order;

(B) provide procedures for the renewal of an extreme risk protection order;

(C) establish burdens and standards of proof for issuance of orders described in this subsection that are substantially similar or higher than the burdens and standards of proof set forth in this subsection;

(D) limit the individuals who may submit an application described in this subsection; and

(E) include other authorizations or requirements the State or tribal authorities deem appropriate.

SEC. 402. FEDERAL EXTREME RISK PROTEC-

TION ORDERS.

(a) In General.—Chapter 44 of title 18, United States Code, as amended by section 101 of this Act, is amended by adding at the end the following:

"§ 933. Extreme risk protection orders

"(a) Definitions.—In this section:

"(1) COURT.—The term 'court' means a district court of the United States.

"(2) DESIGNATED LAW ENFORCEMENT OF-FICER.—The term 'designated law enforcement officer' means a law enforcement officer, designated by a United States marshal, who agrees to receive firearms, ammunition, and permit, as applicable, surrendered under subsection (f).

"(3) DIRECTOR.—The term 'Director' means the Director of the Administrative Office of the United States Courts.

"(4) EX PARTE EXTREME RISK PROTECTION ORDER; EX PARTE ORDER.—The term 'ex parte extreme risk protection order' or 'ex parte order' means an extreme risk protection order issued under subsection (c).

"(5) EXTREME RISK PROTECTION ORDER.—

The term 'extreme risk protection order'—

"(A) means an order issued by a Federal court under this section, the primary purpose of which is to reduce the risk of firearm-related death or injury by enjoining an individual from purchasing, possessing, or receiving, in or affecting interstate and foreign commerce, a firearm or ammunition; and

"(B) does not include a domestic violence protection order, as defined in section 2266.

"(6) FAMILY OR HOUSEHOLD MEMBER.—The term 'family or household member', with respect to a respondent, means any—

"(A) parent, spouse, sibling, or child related by blood, marriage, or adoption to the respondent;

"(B) dating partner of the respondent;

"(C) individual who has a child in common with the respondent, regardless of whether the individual has—

"(i) been married to the respondent; or

"(ii) lived together with the respondent at any time;

"(D) individual who resides or has resided with the

respondent during the past year;

"(E) domestic partner of the respondent;

"(F) individual who has a legal parent-child relationship with the respondent, including a stepparent-stepchild and grandparent-grandchild relationship; or

"(G) individual who is acting or has acted as the legal guardian of the respondent.

"(7) LAW ENFORCEMENT OFFICER.—The term 'law enforcement officer' means any officer, agent, or employee of the Federal Government or a State government, unit of local government, or Indian tribe (as defined in section 4 of the Indian Self-Determination and Education Assistance Act (25 U.S.C. 5304)) authorized—

"(A) by law or by a government agency to engage in or supervise the prevention, detection, or investigation of any violation of criminal law; or

"(B) by law to supervise sentenced criminal offenders.

"(8) LONG-TERM EXTREME RISK PROTECTION ORDER; LONG-TERM ORDER.—The term 'long-term extreme risk protection order' or 'long-term order' means an extreme risk protection order issued under subsection (d).

"(9) MENTAL HEALTH AGENCY.—The term 'mental health agency' means an agency of a State, tribal, or local government or its contracted agency that is responsible for mental health services or co-occurring mental health and substance abuse services.

"(10) NATIONAL INSTANT CRIMINAL BACK-GROUND CHECK SYSTEM.—The term 'national instant criminal background check system' means the national instant criminal background check system established under section 103 of the Brady Handgun Violence Prevention Act (34 U.S.C. 40901).

"(b) Petition.—

"(1) IN GENERAL.—A family or household member of the applicable individual, or a law enforcement officer, may submit to an appropriate district court of the United States a petition requesting that the court issue an ex parte extreme risk protection order or long-term extreme risk protection order with respect to an individual.

"(2) NO FEES.—A court may not charge a petitioner any fee for filing a petition under paragraph (1).

"(3) CONFIDENTIALITY.—A petitioner who is a law enforcement officer may provide the identity of the sources of the petitioner, and any identifying information, to the court under seal.

"(c) Ex Parte Orders.—

"(1) TIMING.—

"(A) IN GENERAL.—Except as provided in subparagraph (B), a court that receives a petition for an ex parte order under subsection (b) shall grant or deny the petition on the date on which the petition is submitted.

"(B) LATE PETITIONS.—If a court receives a petition for an ex parte order submitted under subsection (b) too late in the day to permit effective review, the court shall grant or deny the petition on the next day of judicial business at a time early enough to permit the court to file an order with the clerk of the court during that day.

"(2) EVIDENCE REQUIRED.—Before issuing an ex parte order, a court shall require that the petitioner submit a signed affidavit, sworn to before the court, that—

"(A) explains why the petitioner believes that the

respondent poses a risk of imminent personal injury to the respondent or another individual, by purchasing, possessing, or receiving a firearm or ammunition; and

"(B) describes the interactions and conversations of the petitioner with—

"(i) the respondent; or

"(ii) another individual, if the petitioner believes that information obtained from that individual is credible and reliable.

"(3) STANDARD FOR ISSUANCE OF ORDER.—A court may issue an ex parte order only upon a finding of probable cause to believe that—

"(A) the respondent poses a risk of imminent personal injury to the respondent or another individual, by purchasing, possessing, or receiving a firearm or ammunition; and

"(B) the order is necessary to prevent the injury described in subparagraph (A).

"(4) DURATION.—An ex parte order shall expire on the earlier of—

"(A) the date that is 14 days after the date of issuance; or

"(B) the date on which the court determines whether to issue a long-term order with respect to the respondent.

"(d) Long-Term Orders.—

"(1) HEARING REQUIRED.—If a court receives a petition for an extreme risk protection order for a respondent under subsection (b), the court shall hold a hearing to determine whether to issue a long-term order with respect to the respondent either—

"(A) (i) except as provided in clause (ii), not later than 72 hours after the court issues an ex parte order with respect to the respondent; or

"(ii) if the court issues an ex parte order with respect to the respondent but the order is not served on the respondent within 72 hours of the issuance, not later than 72 hours after the order is served on the respondent; or

"(B) if the respondent waives the right to a hearing under subparagraph (A) or the court does not issue an ex parte order, not later than 14 days after the date on which the court receives the petition.

"(2) NOTICE AND OPPORTUNITY TO BE HEARD.—

"(A) IN GENERAL.—The court shall provide the respondent with notice and the opportunity to be heard at a hearing under this subsection, sufficient to protect the due process rights of the respondent.

"(B) RIGHT TO COUNSEL.—

"(i) IN GENERAL.—At a hearing under this subsection, the respondent may be represented by counsel who is—

"(I) chosen by the respondent; and

"(II) authorized to practice at such a hearing.

"(ii) COURT-PROVIDED COUNSEL.—

"(I) IN GENERAL.—If the respondent is financially unable to obtain representation by counsel, the court, at the request of the respondent, may appoint counsel to represent the respondent in proceedings under this subsection.

"(II) REASONABLE COMPENSATION.—An attorney appointed pursuant to this subparagraph shall be provided reasonable attorney's fees and expenses.

"(3) BURDEN OF PROOF; STANDARD.—At a hearing under this subsection, the petitioner—

"(A) shall have the burden of proving all material facts; and

"(B) shall be required to demonstrate, by a preponderance of the evidence, that—

"(i) the respondent poses a risk of personal injury to the respondent or another individual, during the period to be covered by the proposed extreme risk protection order, by purchasing, possessing, or receiving a firearm or ammunition; and

"(ii) the order is necessary to prevent the injury described in clause (i).

"(4) ISSUANCE.—Upon a showing of clear and convincing evidence under paragraph (3), the court shall issue a long-term order with respect to the respondent that shall be in effect for a period of not more than 180 days.

"(5) DENIAL.—If the court finds that there is not clear and convincing evidence to support the issuance of a long-term order, the court shall dissolve any ex parte order then in effect with respect to the respondent.

"(6) RENEWAL.—

"(A) NOTICE OF SCHEDULED EXPIRATION.—Thirty days before the date on which a long-term order is scheduled to expire, the court that issued the order shall—

"(i) notify the petitioner and the respondent that the order is scheduled to expire; and

"(ii) advise the petitioner and the respondent of the procedures for seeking a renewal of the order under this paragraph.

"(B) PETITION.—If a family or household member of the respondent, or a law enforcement officer, believes that the conditions under paragraph (3)(B) continue to apply with respect to a respondent who is subject to a long-term order, the family or household member or law enforcement officer may submit to the court that issued the order a petition for a renewal of the order.

"(C) HEARING.—A court that receives a petition submitted under subparagraph (B) shall hold a hearing to determine whether to issue a renewed long-term order with respect to the respondent.

"(D) APPLICABLE PROCEDURES.—The requirements under paragraphs (2) through (5) shall apply to the consideration of a petition for a renewed long-term order submitted under subparagraph (B) of this paragraph.

"(E) ISSUANCE.—Upon a showing by clear and convincing evidence that the conditions under paragraph (3)(B) continue to apply with respect to the respondent, the court shall issue a renewed long-term order with respect to the respondent.

"(e) Factors To Consider.—In determining whether to issue an extreme risk protection order, a court—

"(1) shall consider factors including—

"(A) recent threats, by any medium, or acts of violence by the respondent directed toward other individuals;

"(B) recent threats, by any medium, or acts of violence by the respondent directed toward the respondent;

"(C) recent acts of cruelty to animals by the respondent;

"(D) evidence of ongoing abuse of controlled substances or alcohol by the respondent that has led to threats or acts of violence directed toward the respondent or other individuals; and

"(E) evidence of danger to self or others transmitted by electronic communications or publications through social media or networking; and

"(2) may consider other factors, including—

"(A) the reckless use, display, or brandishing of a firearm by the respondent;

"(B) a history of violence or attempted violence by the respondent against other individuals; and

"(C) evidence of explicit or implicit threats made by the person through any medium that demonstrate that the person poses a risk of personal injury to the person or others.

"(f) Relinquishment Of Firearms And Ammunition.—

"(1) ORDER OF SURRENDER.—Upon issuance of an ex parte order or long-term order, the court shall order the respondent to surrender all firearms and ammunition that the respondent possesses or owns, in or affecting interstate commerce, as well as any permit authorizing the respondent to purchase or possess firearms (including a concealed carry permit), to—

"(A) the United States Marshals Service; or

"(B) a designated law enforcement officer.

"(2) SURRENDER AND REMOVAL.—

"(A) MANNER OF SERVICE.—

"(i) PERSONAL SERVICE.—Except as provided in clause (ii), a United States marshal or designated law enforcement officer shall serve an extreme risk protection order on a respondent by handing the order to the respondent.

"(ii) ALTERNATIVE SERVICE.—If the respondent cannot reasonably be located for service as described in clause (i), an extreme risk protection order may be served on the respondent in any manner authorized under the Federal Rules of Civil Procedure.

"(B) REMOVAL.—Except as provided in subparagraph (C), a United States marshal or designated law enforcement officer serving an extreme risk protection order personally on the respondent shall—

"(i) request that all firearms and ammunition, in or affecting interstate commerce, as well as any permit authorizing the respondent to purchase or possess firearms (including a concealed carry permit), that the respondent possesses or owns—

"(I) be immediately surrendered to the United States marshal or designated law enforcement officer; or

"(II) at the option of the respondent, be immediately surrendered and sold to a federally licensed firearms dealer; and

"(ii) take possession of all firearms and ammunition described in clause (i) that are not sold under subclause (II) of that clause, as well as any permit described in that clause, that are—

"(I) surrendered;

"(II) in plain sight; or

"(III) discovered pursuant to a lawful search.

"(C) ALTERNATIVE SURRENDER.—If a United States marshal or designated law enforcement officer is not able to personally serve an extreme risk protection order under subparagraph (A)(i), or is not reasonably able to take custody of the firearms, ammunition, and permits under subparagraph (B), the respondent shall surrender the firearms, ammunition, and permits in a safe manner to the control of a United States marshal or designated law enforcement officer not later than 48 hours after being served with the order.

"(3) RECEIPT.—

"(A) ISSUANCE.—At the time of surrender or removal under paragraph (2), a United States marshal or designated law enforcement officer taking possession of a firearm, ammunition, or a permit pursuant to an extreme risk protection order shall—

"(i) issue a receipt identifying all firearms, ammunition, and permits that have been surrendered or removed; and

"(ii) provide a copy of the receipt issued under clause (i) to the respondent.

"(B) FILING.—Not later than 72 hours after service of an order under paragraph (2)(A), the United States marshal who served the order or designated another law enforcement officer to do so shall—

"(i) file the original receipt issued under subparagraph (A) of this paragraph with the court that issued the extreme risk protection order; and

"(ii) ensure that the United States Marshals Service

retains a copy of the receipt.

"(C) DESIGNATED LAW ENFORCEMENT OF-FICER.—If a designated law enforcement officer issues a receipt under subparagraph (A), the officer shall submit the original receipt and a copy of the receipt to the appropriate United States marshal to enable the United States marshal to comply with subparagraph (B).

"(4) FORFEITURE.—If a respondent knowingly attempts, in violation of an extreme risk protection order, to access a firearm, ammunition, or a permit that was surrendered or removed under this sub-section, the firearm, ammunition, or permit shall be subject to seizure and forfeiture under section 924(d).

"(g) Return Of Firearms And Ammunition.—

"(1) NOTICE.—If an extreme risk protection order is dissolved, or expires and is not renewed, the court that issued the order shall order the United States Marshals Service to—

"(A) confirm, through the national instant criminal background check system and any other relevant law enforcement databases, that the respondent may lawfully own and possess firearms and ammu-nition; and

"(B) (i) if the respondent may lawfully own and possess firearms and ammunition, notify the respondent that the respondent may retrieve each firearm, ammunition, or permit surrendered by or removed from the respondent under subsection (f); or

"(ii) if the respondent may not lawfully own or possess firearms and ammunition, notify the respondent that each firearm, ammunition, or permit surrendered by or removed from the respondent under subsection (f) will be returned only when the respondent demonstrates to the United States Marshals Service that the respondent may lawfully own and possess firearms and ammunition.

"(2) RETURN.—If an extreme risk protection order is dissolved, or expires and is not renewed, and the United States Marshals Service confirms under paragraph (1)(A) that the respondent may lawfully own and possess firearms and ammunition, the court that issued the order shall order the entity that possesses each firearm, ammunition, or permit surrendered by or removed from the respondent under subsection (f) to return those items to the respondent.

"(h) Return Of Firearms And Ammunition Improperly Received.—If a court, in a hearing under subsection (d), determines that a firearm or ammunition surrendered by or removed from a respondent under subsection (f) is owned by an individual other than the respondent, the court may order the United States marshal or designated law enforcement officer in possession of the firearm or ammunition to transfer the firearm or ammunition to that individual if—

"(1) the individual may lawfully own and possess firearms and ammunition; and

"(2) the individual will not provide the respondent with access to the firearm or ammunition.

"(i) Penalty For False Reporting Or Frivolous Petitions.—An individual who knowingly submits materially false information to the court in a petition for an extreme risk protection order under this section, or who knowingly files such a petition that is frivolous, unreasonable, or without foundation, shall be fined not less than $1,000, in addition to any other penalty authorized by law, as the court deems necessary to deter such abuse of process.

"(j) Model Policy.—

"(1) IN GENERAL.—The Director shall draft a model policy to maximize the accessibility of extreme risk protection orders.

"(2) CONTENTS.—In drafting the model policy under paragraph (1), the Director shall—

"(A) ensure that State and local law enforcement officers and members of the public without legal training are able to easily file petitions for extreme risk protection orders;

"(B) prescribe outreach efforts by employees of the district courts of the United States to familiarize relevant law enforcement officers and the public with the procedures for filing petitions, either—

"(i) through direct outreach; or

"(ii) in coordination with—

"(I) relevant officials in the executive or legislative branch of the Federal Government; or

"(II) with State and local officials;

"(C) prescribe policies for allowing the filing of petitions and prompt adjudication of petitions on weekends and outside of normal court hours;

"(D) prescribe policies for coordinating with law enforcement agencies to ensure the safe, timely, and effective service of extreme risk protection orders and relinquishment of firearms, ammunition, and permits, as applicable; and

"(E) identify governmental and non-governmental resources and partners to help officials of the district courts of the United States coordinate with civil society organizations to ensure the safe and effective implementation of this section.

"(k) Reporting.—

"(1) INDIVIDUAL REPORTS.—

"(A) IN GENERAL.—Not later than 2 court days after the date on which a court issues or dissolves an extreme risk protection order under this section or an extreme risk protection order expires without being renewed, the court shall notify—

"(i) the Attorney General;

"(ii) each relevant mental health agency in the State in which the order is issued; and

"(iii) State and local law enforcement officials in the jurisdiction in which the order is issued, including the national instant criminal background check system single point of contact for the State of residence of the respondent, where applicable.

"(B) FORMAT.—A court shall submit a notice under subparagraph (A) in an electronic format, in a manner prescribed by the Attorney General.

"(C) UPDATE OF DATABASES.—As soon as practicable and not later than 5 days after receiving a notice under subparagraph (A), the Attorney General shall update the background check databases of the Attorney General to reflect the prohibitions articulated in the applicable extreme risk protection order.

"(2) ANNUAL REPORTS.—Not later than 1 year after the date of enactment of the Gun Violence Prevention and Community Safety Act of 2020, and annually thereafter, the Director shall submit to the Committee on the Judiciary of the Senate and the Committee on the Judiciary of the House of Representatives a report that includes, with respect to the preceding year—

"(A) the number of petitions for ex parte orders filed, as well as the number of such orders issued and the number denied;

"(B) the number of petitions for long-term orders filed, as well as the number of such orders issued and the number denied;

"(C) the number of petitions for renewals of long-term orders filed, as well as the number of such orders issued and the number denied; and

"(D) the number of cases in which a court has issued a penalty for false reporting or frivolous petitions.

"(l) Authorization Of Appropriations.—There are authorized to be appropriated such sums as are necessary to carry out this section.

"(m) Rule Of Construction.—Nothing in this section may be construed to alter the requirements of subsections (d)(8) or (g)(8) of section 922, relating to domestic violence protective orders.".

(b) Technical And Conforming Amendments.—

(1) TABLE OF SECTIONS.—The table of sections for chapter 44 of title 18, United States Code, as amended by section 101 of this Act, is amended by adding at the end the following:
"933. Extreme risk protection orders.".
(2) FORFEITURE.—Section 924(d)(3) of title 18, United States Code, is amended—

(A) in subparagraph (E), by striking "and" at the end;

(B) in subparagraph (F), by striking the period and

inserting "; and"; and

(C) by adding at the end the following:
"(G) any attempt to violate an extreme risk protection order issued under section 933.".

SEC. 403. FEDERAL FIREARMS PROHIBITION.

(a) Definition.—Section 921(a) of title 18, United States Code, as amended by this Act, is amended by adding at the end the following:
"(53) The term 'extreme risk protection order' has the meaning given the term in section 401 of the Gun Violence Prevention and Community Safety Act of 2020.".

(b) Prohibitions.—Section 922 of title 18, United States Code, is amended—

(1) in subsection (d), as amended by section 301 of this Act, by adding at the end the following:
"(11) is subject to an extreme risk protection order."; and

(2) in subsection (g), as amended by section 301 of this Act, by adding at the end the following:
"(11) is subject to an extreme risk protection order,".

SEC. 404. IDENTIFICATION RECORDS.

Section 534 of title 28, United States Code, is

amended—

(1) in subsection (a)—

(A) in paragraph (3), by striking "and" at the end; and

(B) by redesignating paragraph (4) as paragraph (5); and

(C) by inserting after paragraph (3) the following: "(4) acquire, collect, classify, and preserve records from Federal, tribal, and State courts and other agencies identifying individuals subject to extreme risk protection orders, as defined in section 401 of the Gun Violence Prevention and Community Safety Act of 2020, provided that such records shall be destroyed if the orders expire or are terminated or dissolved; and";

(2) in subsection (b), by striking "(a)(4)" and inserting "(a)(5)"; and

(3) by adding at the end the following:

"(g) Federal, tribal, and State criminal justice agencies and criminal and civil courts may—

"(1) include extreme risk protection orders, as defined in section 401 of the Gun Violence Prevention and Community Safety Act of 2020, in national crime information databases, as defined in subsection (f)(3) of this section; and

"(2) have access to information regarding extreme risk protection orders through the national crime information databases, as defined in subsection (f)(3) of this section.".

SEC. 405. CONFORMING AMENDMENT.
Section 3(1) of the NICS Improvement Amendments Act of 2007 (34 U.S.C. 40903(1)) is amended by striking "section 922(g)(8)" and inserting "paragraph (8) or (11) of section 922(g)".

SEC. 406. FULL FAITH AND CREDIT.
Any extreme risk protection order issued under a State or Tribal law enacted in accordance with this title shall be accorded the same full faith and credit by the court of another State, Indian Tribe, or unit of local government (the enforcing State, Indian Tribe, or unit of local government) and enforced by the court and law enforcement personnel of the other State, Tribal, or local government as if it were the order of the enforcing State, Indian Tribe, or unit of local government.

TITLE V—ASSAULT WEAPONS AND FIREARMS SILENCERS AND MUFFLERS BAN
Subtitle A—Assault Weapons Ban

SEC. 511. DEFINITIONS.

(a) In General.—Section 921(a) of title 18, United States Code, is amended—

(1) by inserting after paragraph (29) the following:
"(30) The term 'semiautomatic pistol' means any repeating pistol that—

"(A) utilizes a portion of the energy of a firing cartridge to extract the fired cartridge case and chamber the next round; and

"(B) requires a separate pull of the trigger to fire each cartridge.

"(31) The term 'semiautomatic shotgun' means any repeating shotgun that—

"(A) utilizes a portion of the energy of a firing cartridge to extract the fired cartridge case and chamber the next round; and

"(B) requires a separate pull of the trigger to fire each cartridge."; and

(2) by adding at the end the following:
"(37) The term 'semiautomatic assault weapon' means any of the following, regardless of country of manufacture or caliber of ammunition accepted:

"(A) A semiautomatic rifle that has the capacity to accept a detachable magazine and any 1 of the following:

"(i) A pistol grip.

"(ii) A forward grip.

"(iii) A folding, telescoping, or detachable stock, or is otherwise foldable or adjustable in a manner that operates to reduce the length, size, or any other dimension, or otherwise enhances the concealability, of the weapon.

"(iv) A grenade launcher.

"(v) A barrel shroud.

"(vi) A threaded barrel.

"(B) A semiautomatic rifle that has a fixed magazine with the capacity to accept more than 10 rounds, except for an attached tubular device designed to accept, and capable of operating only with, .22 caliber rimfire ammunition.

"(C) Any part, combination of parts, component, device, attachment, or accessory that is designed or functions to accelerate the rate of fire of a semiautomatic rifle but not convert the semiautomatic rifle into a machinegun.

"(D) A semiautomatic pistol that has the capacity to accept a detachable magazine and any 1 of the following:

"(i) A threaded barrel.

"(ii) A second pistol grip.

"(iii) A barrel shroud.

"(iv) The capacity to accept a detachable magazine at some location outside of the pistol grip.

"(v) A semiautomatic version of an automatic firearm.

"(vi) A manufactured weight of 50 ounces or more when unloaded.

"(vii) A stabilizing brace or similar component.

"(E) A semiautomatic pistol with a fixed magazine that has the capacity to accept more than 10 rounds.

"(F) A semiautomatic shotgun that has any 1 of the following:

"(i) A folding, telescoping, or detachable stock.

"(ii) A pistol grip.

"(iii) A fixed magazine with the capacity to accept more than 5 rounds.

"(iv) The ability to accept a detachable magazine.

"(v) A forward grip.

"(vi) A grenade launcher.

"(G) Any shotgun with a revolving cylinder.

"(H) All of the following rifles, copies, duplicates, variants, or altered facsimiles with the capability of any such weapon thereof:

"(i) All AK types, including the following:

"(I) AK, AK47, AK47S, AK–74, AKM, AKS, ARM, MAK90, MISR, NHM90, NHM91, Rock River Arms LAR–47, SA85, SA93, Vector Arms AK–47, VEPR, WASR–10, and WUM.

"(II) IZHMASH Saiga AK.

"(III) MAADI AK47 and ARM.

"(IV) Norinco 56S, 56S2, 84S, and 86S.

"(V) Poly Technologies AK47 and AKS.

"(ii) All AR types, including the following:

"(I) AR–10.

"(II) AR–15.

"(III) Alexander Arms Overmatch Plus 16.

"(IV) Armalite M15 22LR Carbine.

"(V) Armalite M15–T.

"(VI) Barrett REC7.

"(VII) Beretta AR–70.

"(VIII) Black Rain Ordnance Recon Scout.

"(IX) Bushmaster ACR.

"(X) Bushmaster Carbon 15.

"(XI) Bushmaster MOE series.

"(XII) Bushmaster XM15.

"(XIII) Chiappa Firearms MFour rifles.

"(XIV) Colt Match Target rifles.

"(XV) CORE Rifle Systems CORE15 rifles.

"(XVI) Daniel Defense M4A1 rifles.

"(XVII) Devil Dog Arms 15 Series rifles.

"(XVIII) Diamondback DB15 rifles.

"(XIX) DoubleStar AR rifles.

"(XX) DPMS Tactical rifles.

"(XXI) DSA Inc. ZM–4 Carbine.

"(XXII) Heckler & Koch MR556.

"(XXIII) High Standard HSA–15 rifles.

"(XXIV) Jesse James Nomad AR–15 rifle.

"(XXV) Knight's Armament SR–15.

"(XXVI) Lancer L15 rifles.

"(XXVII) MGI Hydra Series rifles.

"(XXVIII) Mossberg MMR Tactical rifles.

"(XXIX) Noreen Firearms BN 36 rifle.

"(XXX) Olympic Arms.

"(XXXI) POF USA P415.

"(XXXII) Precision Firearms AR rifles.

"(XXXIII) Remington R–15 rifles.

"(XXXIV) Rhino Arms AR rifles.

"(XXXV) Rock River Arms LAR–15.

"(XXXVI) Sig Sauer SIG516 rifles and MCX rifles.

"(XXXVII) SKS with a detachable magazine.

"(XXXVIII) Smith & Wesson M&P15 rifles.

"(XXXIX) Stag Arms AR rifles.

"(XL) Sturm, Ruger & Co. SR556 and AR–556 rifles.

"(XLI) Uselton Arms Air-Lite M–4 rifles.

"(XLII) Windham Weaponry AR rifles.

"(XLIII) WMD Guns Big Beast.

"(XLIV) Yankee Hill Machine Company, Inc. YHM–15 rifles.

"(iii) Barrett M107A1.

"(iv) Barrett M82A1.

"(v) Beretta CX4 Storm.

"(vi) Calico Liberty Series.

"(vii) CETME Sporter.

"(viii) Daewoo K–1, K–2, Max 1, Max 2, AR 100, and AR 110C.

"(ix) Fabrique Nationale/FN Herstal FAL, LAR, 22 FNC, 308 Match, L1A1 Sporter, PS90, SCAR, and FS2000.

"(x) Feather Industries AT–9.

"(xi) Galil Model AR and Model ARM.

"(xii) Hi-Point Carbine.

"(xiii) HK–91, HK–93, HK–94, HK–PSG–1, and HK USC.

"(xiv) IWI TAVOR, Galil ACE rifle.

"(xv) Kel-Tec Sub-2000, SU–16, and RFB.

"(xvi) SIG AMT, SIG PE–57, Sig Sauer SG 550, Sig Sauer SG 551, and SIG MCX.

"(xvii) Springfield Armory SAR–48.

"(xviii) Steyr AUG.

"(xix) Sturm, Ruger & Co. Mini-14 Tactical Rifle M–14/20CF.

"(xx) All Thompson rifles, including the following:

"(I) Thompson M1SB.

"(II) Thompson T1100D.

"(III) Thompson T150D.

"(IV) Thompson T1B.

"(V) Thompson T1B100D.

"(VI) Thompson T1B50D.

"(VII) Thompson T1BSB.

"(VIII) Thompson T1–C.

"(IX) Thompson T1D.

"(X) Thompson T1SB.

"(XI) Thompson T5.

"(XII) Thompson T5100D.

"(XIII) Thompson TM1.

"(XIV) Thompson TM1C.

"(xxi) UMAREX UZI rifle.

"(xxii) UZI Mini Carbine, UZI Model A Carbine, and UZI Model B Carbine.

"(xxiii) Valmet M62S, M71S, and M78.

"(xxiv) Vector Arms UZI Type.

"(xxv) Weaver Arms Nighthawk.

"(xxvi) Wilkinson Arms Linda Carbine.

"(I) All of the following pistols, copies, duplicates, variants, or altered facsimiles with the capability of any such weapon thereof:

"(i) All AK–47 types, including the following:

"(I) Centurion 39 AK pistol.

"(II) CZ Scorpion pistol.

"(III) Draco AK–47 pistol.

"(IV) HCR AK–47 pistol.

"(V) IO Inc. Hellpup AK–47 pistol.

"(VI) Krinkov pistol.

"(VII) Mini Draco AK–47 pistol.

"(VIII) PAP M92 pistol.

"(IX) Yugo Krebs Krink pistol.

"(ii) All AR–15 types, including the following:

"(I) American Spirit AR–15 pistol.

"(II) Bushmaster Carbon 15 pistol.

"(III) Chiappa Firearms M4 Pistol GEN II.

"(IV) CORE Rifle Systems CORE15 Roscoe pistol.

"(V) Daniel Defense MK18 pistol.

"(VI) DoubleStar Corporation AR pistol.

"(VII) DPMS AR–15 pistol.

"(VIII) Jesse James Nomad AR–15 pistol.

"(IX) Olympic Arms AR–15 pistol.

"(X) Osprey Armament MK–18 pistol.

"(XI) POF USA AR pistols.

"(XII) Rock River Arms LAR 15 pistol.

"(XIII) Uselton Arms Air-Lite M–4 pistol.

"(iii) Calico Liberty pistols.

"(iv) DSA SA58 PKP FAL pistol.

"(v) Encom MP–9 and MP–45.

"(vi) Heckler & Koch model SP–89 pistol.

"(vii) Intratec AB–10, TEC–22 Scorpion, TEC–9, and TEC–DC9.

"(viii) IWI Galil Ace pistol, UZI PRO pistol.

"(ix) Kel-Tec PLR 16 pistol.

"(x) The following MAC types:

"(I) MAC–10.

"(II) MAC–11.

"(III) Masterpiece Arms MPA A930 Mini Pistol, MPA460 Pistol, MPA Tactical Pistol, and MPA Mini Tactical Pistol.

"(IV) Military Armament Corp. Ingram M–11.

"(V) Velocity Arms VMAC.

"(xi) Sig Sauer P556 pistol.

"(xii) Sites Spectre.

"(xiii) All Thompson types, including the following:

"(I) Thompson TA510D.

"(II) Thompson TA5.

"(xiv) All UZI types, including Micro-UZI.

"(J) All of the following shotguns, copies, duplicates, variants, or altered facsimiles with the capability of any such weapon thereof:

"(i) DERYA Anakon MC–1980, Anakon SD12.

"(ii) Doruk Lethal shotguns.

"(iii) Franchi LAW–12 and SPAS 12.

"(iv) All IZHMASH Saiga 12 types, including the following:

"(I) IZHMASH Saiga 12.

"(II) IZHMASH Saiga 12S.

"(III) IZHMASH Saiga 12S EXP–01.

"(IV) IZHMASH Saiga 12K.

"(V) IZHMASH Saiga 12K–030.

"(VI) IZHMASH Saiga 12K–040 Taktika.

"(v) Streetsweeper.

"(vi) Striker 12.

"(K) All belt-fed semiautomatic firearms, including TNW M2HB and FN M2495.

"(L) Any combination of parts from which a firearm described in subparagraphs (A) through (K) can be assembled.

"(M) The frame or receiver of a rifle or shotgun described in subparagraph (A), (B), (C), (F), (G), (H), (J), or (K).

"(38) The term 'large capacity ammunition feeding device'—

"(A) means a magazine, belt, drum, feed strip, or similar device, including any such device joined or coupled with another in any manner, that has an overall capacity of, or that can be readily restored, changed, or converted to accept, more than 10 rounds of ammunition; and

"(B) does not include an attached tubular device designed to accept, and capable of operating only with, .22 caliber rimfire ammunition.".

(b) Related Definitions.—Section 921(a) of title 18, United States Code, as amended by this Act, is amended by adding at the end the following:
"(39) The term 'barrel shroud'—

"(A) means a shroud that is attached to, or partially or completely encircles, the barrel of a firearm so that the shroud protects the user of the firearm from heat generated by the barrel; and

"(B) does not include—

"(i) a slide that partially or completely encloses the barrel; or

"(ii) an extension of the stock along the bottom of the barrel which does not encircle or substantially encircle the barrel.

"(40) The term 'detachable magazine' means an ammunition feeding device that can be removed from a firearm without disassembly of the firearm action.

"(41) The term 'fixed magazine' means an ammunition feeding device that is permanently fixed to the firearm in such a manner that it cannot be removed without disassembly of the firearm.

"(42) The term 'folding, telescoping, or detachable stock' means a stock that folds, telescopes, detaches or otherwise operates to reduce the length, size, or any other dimension, or otherwise enhances the concealability, of a firearm.

"(43) The term 'forward grip' means a grip located

forward of the trigger that functions as a pistol grip.

"(44) The term 'grenade launcher' means an attachment for use on a firearm that is designed to propel a grenade or other similar destructive device.

"(45) The term 'permanently inoperable' means a firearm which is incapable of discharging a shot by means of an explosive and incapable of being readily restored to a firing condition.

"(46) The term 'pistol grip' means a grip, a thumbhole stock or Thordsen-type grip or stock, or any other characteristic that can function as a grip.

"(47) The term 'threaded barrel' means a feature or characteristic that is designed in such a manner to allow for the attachment of a device such as a firearm silencer or a flash suppressor.

"(48) The term 'qualified law enforcement officer' has the meaning given the term in section 926B.

"(49) The term 'grandfathered semiautomatic assault weapon' means any semiautomatic assault weapon the importation, possession, sale, or transfer of which would be unlawful under section 922(v) but for the exception under paragraph (2) of such section.

"(50) The term 'belt-fed semiautomatic firearm' means any repeating firearm that—

"(A) utilizes a portion of the energy of a firing cartridge to extract the fired cartridge case and chamber the next round;

"(B) requires a separate pull of the trigger to fire each cartridge; and

"(C) has the capacity to accept a belt ammunition feeding device.".

SEC. 512. RESTRICTIONS ON ASSAULT WEAPONS AND LARGE CAPACITY AMMUNITION FEEDING DEVICES.

(a) In General.—Section 922 of title 18, United States Code, is amended—

(1) by inserting after subsection (u) the following:
"(v) (1) It shall be unlawful for a person to import, sell, manufacture, transfer, or possess, in or affecting interstate or foreign commerce, a semiautomatic assault weapon.

"(2) Paragraph (1) shall not apply to the possession, sale, or transfer of any semiautomatic assault weapon otherwise lawfully possessed under Federal law on the date of enactment of the Gun Violence Prevention and Community Safety Act of 2020.

"(3) Paragraph (1) shall not apply to any firearm that—

"(A) is manually operated by bolt, pump, lever, or slide action;

"(B) has been rendered permanently inoperable; or

"(C) is an antique firearm, as defined in section 921 of this title.

"(4) Paragraph (1) shall not apply to—

"(A) the importation for, manufacture for, sale to, transfer to, or possession by the United States or a department or agency of the United States or a State or a department, agency, or political subdivision of a State, or a sale or transfer to or possession by a qualified law enforcement officer employed by the United States or a department or agency of the United States or a State or a department, agency, or political subdivision of a State, for purposes of law enforcement (whether on or off duty), or a sale or transfer to or possession by a campus law enforcement officer for purposes of law enforcement (whether on or off duty);

"(B) the importation for, or sale or transfer to a licensee under title I of the Atomic Energy Act of

1954 for purposes of establishing and maintaining an on-site physical protection system and security organization required by Federal law, or possession by an employee or contractor of such licensee on-site for such purposes or off-site for purposes of licensee-authorized training or transportation of nuclear materials;

"(C) the possession, by an individual who is retired in good standing from service with a law enforcement agency and is not otherwise prohibited from receiving a firearm, of a semiautomatic assault weapon—

"(i) sold or transferred to the individual by the agency upon such retirement; or

"(ii) that the individual purchased, or otherwise obtained, for official use before such retirement;

"(D) the importation, sale, manufacture, transfer, or possession of a semiautomatic assault weapon by a licensed manufacturer or licensed importer for the purposes of testing or experimentation authorized by the Attorney General; or

"(E) the importation, sale, manufacture, transfer, or possession of a firearm specified in Appendix A to this section, as such firearm was manufactured on the date of introduction of the Gun Violence Prevention and Community Safety Act of 2020.

"(5) For purposes of paragraph (4)(A), the term 'campus law enforcement officer' means an individual who is—

"(A) employed by a private institution of higher education that is eligible for funding under title IV of the Higher Education Act of 1965 (20 U.S.C. 1070 et seq.);

"(B) responsible for the prevention or investigation of crime involving injury to persons or property, including apprehension or detention of persons for such crimes;

"(C) authorized by Federal, State, or local law to carry a firearm, execute search warrants, and make arrests; and

"(D) recognized, commissioned, or certified by a government entity as a law enforcement officer.

"(6) The Attorney General shall establish and maintain, in a timely manner, a record of the make, model, and, if available, date of manufacture of any semiautomatic assault weapon which the Attorney General is made aware has been used in relation to a crime under Federal or State law, and the nature and circumstances of the crime involved, including the outcome of relevant criminal investigations and proceedings. The Attorney General shall annually submit a copy of the record established under this paragraph to the Congress and make the record available to the general public.

"(w) (1) It shall be unlawful for a person to import, sell, manufacture, transfer, or possess, in or affecting interstate or foreign commerce, a large capacity ammunition feeding device.

"(2) Paragraph (1) shall not apply to the possession of any large capacity ammunition feeding device otherwise lawfully possessed on or before the date of enactment of the Gun Violence Prevention and Community Safety Act of 2020.

"(3) Paragraph (1) shall not apply to—

"(A) the importation for, manufacture for, sale to, transfer to, or possession by the United States or a department or agency of the United States or a State or a department, agency, or political subdivision of a State, or a sale or transfer to or possession by a qualified law enforcement officer employed by the United States or a department or agency of the United States or a State or a department, agency, or political subdivision of a State for purposes of law enforcement (whether on or off duty), or a sale or transfer to or possession by a campus law enforcement officer for purposes of law enforcement (whether on or off duty);

"(B) the importation for, or sale or transfer to a licensee under title I of the Atomic Energy Act of 1954 for purposes of establishing and maintaining an on-site physical protection system and security organization required by Federal law, or possession by an employee or contractor of such licensee on-site for such purposes or off-site for purposes of licensee-authorized training or transportation of nuclear materials;

"(C) the possession, by an individual who is retired in good standing from service with a law enforcement agency and is not otherwise prohibited from receiving ammunition, of a large capacity ammunition feeding device—

"(i) sold or transferred to the individual by the agency upon such retirement; or

"(ii) that the individual purchased, or otherwise obtained, for official use before such retirement; or

"(D) the importation, sale, manufacture, transfer, or possession of any large capacity ammunition feeding device by a licensed manufacturer or licensed importer for the purposes of testing or experimentation authorized by the Attorney General.

"(4) For purposes of paragraph (3)(A), the term 'campus law enforcement officer' means an individual who is—

"(A) employed by a private institution of higher education that is eligible for funding under title IV of the Higher Education Act of 1965 (20 U.S.C. 1070 et seq.);

"(B) responsible for the prevention or investigation of crime involving injury to persons or property, including apprehension or detention of persons for such crimes;

"(C) authorized by Federal, State, or local law to carry a firearm, execute search warrants, and make arrests; and

"(D) recognized, commissioned, or certified by a government entity as a law enforcement officer.";
and

(2) by adding at the end the following:
"(aa) Secure Storage Or Safety Device Requirement For Grandfathered Semiautomatic Assault Weapons.—It shall be unlawful for any person, other than a licensed importer, licensed manufacturer, or licensed dealer, to store or keep under the dominion or control of that person any grandfathered semi-

automatic assault weapon that the person knows, or has reasonable cause to believe, will be accessible to an individual prohibited from receiving or possessing a firearm under subsection (g), (n), or (x), or any provision of State law, unless the grandfathered semiautomatic assault weapon is—

"(1) carried on the person, or within such close proximity that the person can readily retrieve and use the grandfathered semiautomatic assault weapon as if the grandfathered semiautomatic assault weapon were carried on the person; or

"(2) locked by a secure gun storage or safety device that the prohibited individual has no ability to access.".

(b) Identification Markings For Semiautomatic Assault Weapons.—Section 923(i) of title 18, United States Code, is amended by adding at the end the following: "The serial number of any semiautomatic assault weapon manufactured after the date of enactment of the Gun Violence Prevention and Community Safety Act of 2020 shall clearly show the date on which the weapon was manufactured or made, legibly and conspicuously engraved or cast on the weapon, and such other identification as the Attorney General shall by regulations prescribe.".

(c) Identification Markings For Large Capacity

Ammunition Feeding Devices.—Section 923(i) of title 18, United States Code, as amended by this Act, is amended by adding at the end the following: "A large capacity ammunition feeding device manufactured after the date of enactment of the Gun Violence Prevention and Community Safety Act of 2020 shall be identified by a serial number and the date on which the device was manufactured or made, legibly and conspicuously engraved or cast on the device, and such other identification as the Attorney General shall by regulations prescribe.".

(d) Seizure And Forfeiture Of Large Capacity Ammunition Feeding Devices.—Subsection (d) of section 924 of title 18, United States Code, is amended—

(1) in paragraph (1)—

(A) by inserting "or large capacity ammunition feeding device" after "firearm or ammunition" each time it appears;

(B) by inserting "or large capacity ammunition feeding device" after "firearms or ammunition" each time it appears; and

(C) by striking "or (k)" and inserting "(k), (r), (v), or (w)";

(2) in paragraph (2)—

(A) in subparagraph (C), by inserting "or large capacity ammunition feeding devices" after "firearms or quantities of ammunition"; and

(3) in paragraph (3)—

(A) in subparagraph (E), by inserting "922(r), 922(v), 922(w)," after "922(n),".

(e) Appendix A.—Section 922 of title 18, United States Code, is amended by adding at the end the following:

APPENDIX A—FIREARMS EXEMPTED BY THE ASSAULT WEAPONS BAN OF 2017

Centerfire Rifles—Autoloaders

"Benelli R1 Rifle
"Browning BAR Mark II Safari Magnum Rifle
"Browning BAR Mark II Safari Semi-Auto Rifle
"Browning BAR Stalker Rifles
"Browning High-Power Rifle
"Browning Longtrac Rifle
"Browning Shorttrac Rifle
"Heckler & Koch HK630
"Heckler & Koch HK770
"Heckler & Koch HK940

"Heckler & Koch Model 300 Rifle

"Heckler & Koch SL7 Rifle

"Iver Johnson 50th Anniversary M–1 Carbine (w/o folding stock)

"Iver Johnson M–1 Carbine (w/o folding stock)

"M–1 Carbines with standard fixed stock

"M–1 Garand with fixed 8 round capacity and standard stock

"Marlin Model 9 Camp Carbine

"Marlin Model 45 Carbine

"Remington Model 74

"Remington Model 81

"Remington Model 740

"Remington Model 742

"Remington Model 750 Synthetic

"Remington Model 750 Woodmaster

"Remington Model 7400 Rifle

"Remington Model 7400 Special Purpose Auto Rifle

"Remington Nylon 66 Auto-Loading Rifle

"Ruger Mini 30

"Ruger Mini-14 (w/o folding or telescoping stock or pistol grip)

"Ruger PC4

"Ruger PC9

"SKS type rifles with fixed 10 round magazine and standard fixed stock

"Winchester Model SXR

Centerfire Rifles—Lever & Slide

"Action Arms Timber Wolf Pump Action
"Beretta 1873 Renegade Lever Action
"Beretta Gold Rush Slide Action
"Big Horn Armory Model 89
"Browning BLR Model 181 Lever Action, All Models
"Browning BPR Pump Rifle
"Browning Model 53 Lever Action
"Browning Model 65 Grade 1 Lever Action Rifle
"Browning Model 71 Rifle and Carbine
"Browning Model 81 BLR
"Browning Model 81 BLR Lever-Action Rifle
"Browning Model 81 Long Action BLR
"Browning Model 1886 High Grade Carbine
"Browning Model 1886 Lever-Action Carbine
"Browning Model B–92 Carbine
"Charles Daly Model 1892 Lever Action, All Models
"Chiappa 1886 Lever Action Rifles
"Cimarron 1860 Henry Replica
"Cimarron 1866 Winchester Replicas
"Cimarron 1873 308 Express Rifle
"Cimarron 1873 Short Rifle
"Cimarron 1873 Sporting Rifle
"Cimarron 1873 Winchester Replicas
"Dixie Engraved 1873 Rifle
"Dixie Lightning Rifle and Carbines
"E.M.F. 1860 Henry Rifle
"E.M.F. 1866 Yellowboy Lever Actions
"E.M.F. Model 73 Lever-Action Rifle
"E.M.F. Model 1873 Lever Actions

"Henry .30/30 Lever Action Carbine
"Henry Big Boy .357 Magnum
"Henry Big Boy .44 Magnum
"Henry Big Boy .45 Colt
"Henry Big Boy Deluxe Engraved .44 Magnum
"Henry Big Boy Deluxe Engraved .45 Colt
"Marlin Model 30AS Lever-Action Carbine
"Marlin Model 62 Lever Action
"Marlin Model 93 Lever Action
"Marlin Model 308MX
"Marlin Model 308MXLR
"Marlin Model 336 Deluxe
"Marlin Model 336C
"Marlin Model 336CS Lever-Action Carbine
"Marlin Model 336DL Lever Action
"Marlin Model 336SS
"Marlin Model 336W
"Marlin Model 336XLR
"Marlin Model 338MX
"Marlin Model 338MXLR
"Marlin Model 444
"Marlin Model 444 Lever-Action
"Marlin Model 444XLR
"Marlin Model 1894 Marlin Model 1894 Cowboy
"Marlin Model 1894 Lever Action, All Models
"Marlin Model 1894C
"Marlin Model 1894CL Classic
"Marlin Model 1894CS Carbine
"Marlin Model 1894S Lever-Action Carbine
"Marlin Model 1894SS

"Marlin Model 1895
"Marlin Model 1895 Cowboy
"Marlin Model 1895 Lever Action, All Models
"Marlin Model 1895G
"Marlin Model 1895GS
"Marlin Model 1895M
"Marlin Model 1895MXLR
"Marlin Model 1895SBL
"Marlin Model 1895SS Lever-Action Rifle
"Marlin Model 1895XLR
"Marlin XLR Lever Action Rifles
"Mitchell 1858 Henry Replica
"Mitchell 1866 Winchester Replica
"Mitchell 1873 Winchester Replica
"Mossberg 464 Lever Action Rifle
"Mossberg Model 472 Lever Action
"Mossberg Model 479 Lever Action
"Navy Arms 1866 Yellowboy Rifle
"Navy Arms 1873 Sporting Rifle
"Navy Arms 1873 Winchester-Style Rifle
"Navy Arms 1892 Short Rifle
"Navy Arms Henry Carbine
"Navy Arms Henry Trapper
"Navy Arms Iron Frame Henry
"Navy Arms Military Henry Rifle
"Puma Bounty Hunter Rifle
"Puma Model 92 Rifles & Carbines
"Remington 7600 Slide Action
"Remington Model 6 Pump Action
"Remington Model 14, 141/2 Pump Actions

"Remington Model 141 Pump Action
"Remington Model 760 Slide Actions
"Remington Model 7600 Special Purpose Slide Action
"Remington Model 7600 Synthetic
"Remington Model 7615 Camo Hunter
"Remington Model 7615 Ranch Carbine
"Remington Model 7615 SPS
"Rossi M92 SRC Saddle-Ring Carbine
"Rossi M92 SRS Short Carbine
"Rossi R92 Lever Action Carbines
"Ruger Model 96/44 Lever Action
"Savage 99C Lever-Action Rifle
"Savage Model 170 Pump Action
"Taurus Thunderbolt Pump Action
"Taylor's & CO., Inc. 1865 Spencer Carbine/Rifle
"Taylor's & CO., Inc. 1892 Carbine/Rifle
"U.S. Fire Arms Standard Lightning Magazine Rifle
"Uberti 1866 Sporting Rifle Uberti 1873 Sporting Rifle
"Uberti 1876 Rifle
"Uberti 1883 Burgess Lever Action Rifle/Carbine
"Uberti Henry Rifle
"Uberti Lightning Rifle/Carbine
"Winchester Lever Actions, All Other Center Fire Models
"Winchester Model 94 Big Bore Side Eject
"Winchester Model 94 Ranger Side Eject Lever-Action Rifle
"Winchester Model 94 Side Eject Lever-Action Rifle

"Winchester Model 94 Trapper Side Eject
"Winchester Model 94 Wrangler Side Eject
"Winchester Model 1895 Safari Centennial

Centerfire Rifles—Bolt Action

"Accurate Arms Raptor & Backpack Bolt Action Rifles
"Alpine Bolt-Action Rifle
"Anschutz 1700D Bavarian Bolt-Action Rifle
"Anschutz 1700D Classic Rifles
"Anschutz 1700D Custom Rifles
"Anschutz 1733D Mannlicher Rifle
"Arnold Arms African Safari & Alaskan Trophy Rifles
"A-Square Caesar Bolt-Action Rifle
"A-Square Genghis Khan Bolt Action Rifle
"A-Square Hamilcar Bolt Action Rifle
"A-Square Hannibal Bolt-Action Rifle
"Auguste Francotte Bolt-Action Rifles
"Bansners Ultimate Bolt Action Rifles
"Beeman/HW 60J Bolt-Action Rifle
"Benton & Brown Firearms, Inc. Model 93 Bolt Action Rifle
"Blackheart International BBG Hunter Bolt Action
"Blackheart International LLC BBG Light Sniper Bolt Action
"Blaser R8 Professional
"Blaser R84 Bolt-Action Rifle
"Blaser R93 Bolt Action Rifle

"BRNO 537 Sporter Bolt-Action Rifle
"BRNO ZKB 527 Fox Bolt-Action Rifle
"BRNO ZKK 600, 601, 602 Bolt-Action Rifles
"Brown Precision Company Bolt Action Sporter
"Browning A-Bolt Gold Medallion
"Browning A-Bolt Left Hand
"Browning A-Bolt Micro Medallion
"Browning A-Bolt Rifle
"Browning A-Bolt Short Action
"Browning A-Bolt Stainless Stalker
"Browning Euro-Bolt Rifle
"Browning High-Power Bolt Action Rifle
"Browning X-Bolt Bolt Action Rifle
"Carbon One Bolt Action Rifle
"Carl Gustaf 2000 Bolt-Action Rifle Century
"Centurion 14 Sporter
"Century Enfield Sporter #4
"Century M70 Sporter
"Century Mauser 98 Sporter
"Century Swedish Sporter #38
"Cheytac M–200
"Cheytac M70 Sporter
"Cooper Model 21 Bolt Action Rifle
"Cooper Model 22 Bolt Action Rifle
"Cooper Model 38 Centerfire Sporter
"Cooper Model 56 Bolt Action Rifle
"CZ 527 Bolt Action Rifles
"CZ 550 Bolt Action Rifles
"CZ 750 Sniper Rifle
"Dakota 22 Sporter Bolt-Action Rifle

"Dakota 76 Classic Bolt-Action Rifle
"Dakota 76 Safari Bolt-Action Rifle
"Dakota 76 Short Action Rifles
"Dakota 97 Bolt Action Rifle
"Dakota 416 Rigby African
"Dakota Predator Rifle
"DSA DS–MP1 Bolt Action Rifle
"E.A.A./Sabatti Rover 870 Bolt-Action Rifle
"EAA/Zastava M–93 Black Arrow Rifle
"Ed Brown Hunting and Model 704 Bolt Action Rifles
"Heym Bolt Action Rifles
"Heym Magnum Express Series Rifle
"Howa Bolt Action Rifles
"Howa Lightning Bolt-Action Rifle
"Howa Realtree Camo Rifle
"H–S Precision Bolt Action Rifles
"Interarms Mark X Bolt Action Rifles
"Interarms Mark X Viscount Bolt-Action Rifle
"Interarms Mark X Whitworth Bolt-Action Rifle
"Interarms Mini-Mark X Rifle
"Interarms Whitworth Express Rifle
"Iver Johnson Model 5100A1 Long-Range Rifle
"KDF K15 American Bolt-Action Rifle
"Kenny Jarrett Bolt Action Rifle
"Kimber Bolt Action Rifles
"Krico Model 600 Bolt-Action Rifle
"Krico Model 700 Bolt-Action Rifles
"Magnum Research Mount Eagle Rifles
"Marlin Model XL7

"Marlin Model XL7C
"Marlin Model XL7L
"Marlin Model XL7W
"Marlin Model XS7
"Marlin Model XS7C
"Marlin Model XS7Y
"Marlin XL–7/XS7 Bolt Action Rifles
"Mauser Model 66 Bolt-Action Rifle
"Mauser Model 99 Bolt-Action Rifle
"McMillan Classic Stainless Sporter
"McMillan Signature Alaskan
"McMillan Signature Classic Sporter
"McMillan Signature Super Varminter
"McMillan Signature Titanium Mountain Rifle
"McMillan Talon Safari Rifle
"McMillan Talon Sporter Rifle
"Merkel KR1 Bolt Action Rifle
"Midland 1500S Survivor Rifle
"Mossberg Model 100 ATR (All-Terrain Rifle)
"Navy Arms TU–33/40 Carbine
"Nosler Model 48 Varmint Rifle
"Parker-Hale Bolt Action Rifles
"Parker-Hale Model 81 Classic African Rifle
"Parker-Hale Model 81 Classic Rifle
"Parker-Hale Model 1000 Rifle
"Parker-Hale Model 1100 Lightweight Rifle
"Parker-Hale Model 1100M African Magnum
"Parker-Hale Model 1200 Super Clip Rifle
"Parker-Hale Model 1200 Super Rifle
"Parker-Hale Model 1300C Scout Rifle

"Parker-Hale Model 2100 Midland Rifle
"Parker-Hale Model 2700 Lightweight Rifle
"Parker-Hale Model 2800 Midland Rifle
"Remington 700 ADL Bolt-Action Rifle
"Remington 700 BDL Bolt-Action Rifle
"Remington 700 BDL European Bolt-Action Rifle
"Remington 700 BDL Left Hand
"Remington 700 BDL SS Rifle
"Remington 700 BDL Varmint Special
"Remington 700 Camo Synthetic Rifle
"Remington 700 Classic Rifle
"Remington 700 Custom KS Mountain Rifle
"Remington 700 Mountain Rifle
"Remington 700 MTRSS Rifle
"Remington 700 Safari
"Remington 700 Stainless Synthetic Rifle
"Remington 700 Varmint Synthetic Rifle
"Remington Model 40–X Bolt Action Rifles
"Remington Model 700 Alaskan Ti
"Remington Model 700 Bolt Action Rifles
"Remington Model 700 CDL
"Remington Model 700 CDL 'Boone and Crockett'
"Remington Model 700 CDL Left-Hand
"Remington Model 700 CDL SF Limited Edition
"Remington Model 700 LSS
"Remington Model 700 Mountain LSS
"Remington Model 700 Sendero SF II
"Remington Model 700 SPS
"Remington Model 700 SPS Buckmasters Edition
"Remington Model 700 SPS Buckmasters Edition

'Young Bucks' Youth
"Remington Model 700 SPS Stainless
"Remington Model 700 SPS Tactical Rifle
"Remington Model 700 SPS Varmint
"Remington Model 700 SPS Varmint (Left-Hand)
"Remington Model 700 SPS Youth Synthetic Left-Hand
"Remington Model 700 VL SS Thumbhole
"Remington Model 700 VLS
"Remington Model 700 VS SF II
"Remington Model 700 VTR
"Remington Model 700 XCR
"Remington Model 700 XCR Camo
"Remington Model 700 XCR Compact Tactical Rifle
"Remington Model 700 XCR Left-Hand
"Remington Model 700 XCR Tactical Long Range Rifle
"Remington Model 715
"Remington Model 770
"Remington Model 770 Bolt Action Rifles
"Remington Model 770 Stainless Camo
"Remington Model 770 Youth
"Remington Model 798
"Remington Model 798 Safari
"Remington Model 798 SPS
"Remington Model 799
"Remington Model Seven 25th Anniversary
"Remington Model Seven Bolt Action Rifles
"Remington Model Seven CDL
"Remington Model Seven Custom KS

"Remington Model Seven Custom MS Rifle
"Remington Model Seven Predator
"Remington Model Seven Youth Rifle
"Ruger M77 Hawkeye African
"Ruger M77 Hawkeye Alaskan
"Ruger M77 Hawkeye All-Weather
"Ruger M77 Hawkeye All-Weather Ultra Light
"Ruger M77 Hawkeye Compact
"Ruger M77 Hawkeye International
"Ruger M77 Hawkeye Laminate Compact
"Ruger M77 Hawkeye Laminate Left-Handed
"Ruger M77 Hawkeye Predator
"Ruger M77 Hawkeye Sporter
"Ruger M77 Hawkeye Standard
"Ruger M77 Hawkeye Standard Left-Handed
"Ruger M77 Hawkeye Tactical
"Ruger M77 Hawkeye Ultra Light
"Ruger M77 Mark II All-Weather Stainless Rifle
"Ruger M77 Mark II Express Rifle
"Ruger M77 Mark II Magnum Rifle
"Ruger M77 Mark II Rifle
"Ruger M77 Mark II Target Rifle
"Ruger M77 RSI International Carbine
"Ruger M77
"Ruger Compact Magnum
"Ruger M77RL Ultra Light
"Ruger M77VT Target Rifle
"Ruger Model 77 Bolt Action Rifles
"Sako Bolt Action Rifles
"Sako Classic Bolt Action

"Sako Deluxe Lightweight
"Sako FiberClass Sporter
"Sako Hunter Left-Hand Rifle
"Sako Hunter LS Rifle Sako Hunter Rifle
"Sako Mannlicher-Style Carbine
"Sako Safari Grade Bolt Action
"Sako Super Deluxe Sporter
"Sako TRG–S Bolt-Action Rifle
"Sako Varmint Heavy Barrel
"Sauer 90 Bolt-Action Rifle
"Savage 16/116 Rifles
"Savage 110 Bolt Action Rifles
"Savage 110CY Youth/Ladies Rifle
"Savage 110F Bolt-Action Rifle
"Savage 110FP Police Rifle
"Savage 110FXP3 Bolt-Action Rifle
"Savage 110G Bolt-Action Rifle
"Savage 110GV Varmint Rifle
"Savage 110GXP3 Bolt-Action Rifle
"Savage 110WLE One of One Thousand Limited
Edition Rifle
"Savage 112 Bolt Action Rifles
"Savage 112FV Varmint Rifle
"Savage 116 Bolt Action Rifles
"Savage 116FSS Bolt-Action Rifle
"Savage Axis Series Bolt Action Rifles
"Savage Model 10 Bolt Action Rifles
"Savage Model 10GXP Package Guns
"Savage Model 11/111 Series Bolt Action Rifles
"Savage Model 12 Series Rifles

"Savage Model 14/114 Rifles
"Savage Model 25 Bolt Action Rifles
"Savage Model 110GXP3 Package Guns
"Savage Model 112BV Heavy Barrel Varmint Rifle
"Savage Model 112FVS Varmint Rifle
"Savage Model 116FSK Kodiak Rifle
"Shilen Rifles Inc. DGA Bolt Action Rifles
"Smith & Wesson i-Bolt Rifle
"Steyr Scout Bolt Action Rifle
"Steyr SSG 69 PII Bolt Action Rifle
"Steyr SSG08 Bolt Action Rifle
"Steyr-Mannlicher Luxus Model L, M, S
"Steyr-Mannlicher Model M Professional Rifle
"Steyr-Mannlicher Sporter Models SL, L, M, S, S/T
"Thompson/Center ICON Bolt Action Rifles
"Thompson/Center Icon Classic Long Action Rifle
"Thompson/Center Icon Medium Action Rifle
"Thompson/Center Icon Precision Hunter
"Thompson/Center Icon Weather Shield Long Action Rifle
"Thompson/Center Icon Weather Shield Medium Action Rifle
"Thompson/Center Venture
"Tikka Bolt-Action Rifle
"Tikka Premium Grade Rifles
"Tikka T3 Bolt Action Rifles
"Tikka Varmint/Continental Rifle
"Tikka Whitetail/Battue Rifle
"Ultra Light Arms Model 20 Rifle
"Ultra Light Arms Model 24

"Ultra Light Arms Model 28, Model 40 Rifles
"Voere Model 2155, 2150 Bolt-Action Rifles
"Voere Model 2165 Bolt-Action Rifle
"Voere VEC 91 Lightning Bolt-Action Rifle
"Weatherby Classicmark No. 1 Rifle
"Weatherby Lasermark V Rifle
"Weatherby Mark V Crown Custom Rifles
"Weatherby Mark V Deluxe Bolt-Action Rifle
"Weatherby Mark V Rifles
"Weatherby Mark V Safari Grade Custom Rifles
"Weatherby Mark V Sporter Rifle
"Weatherby Vanguard Bolt Action Rifles
"Weatherby Vanguard Classic No. 1 Rifle
"Weatherby Vanguard Classic Rifle
"Weatherby Vanguard VGX Deluxe Rifle
"Weatherby Vanguard Weatherguard Rifle
"Weatherby Weatherguard Alaskan Rifle
"Weatherby Weathermark Alaskan Rifle
"Weatherby Weathermark Rifle
"Weatherby Weathermark Rifles
"Wichita Classic Rifle
"Wichita Varmint Rifle
"Winchester Model 70 Bolt Action Rifles
"Winchester Model 70 Custom Sharpshooter
"Winchester Model 70 Custom Sporting Sharp-
shooter Rifle
"Winchester Model 70 DBM Rifle
"Winchester Model 70 DBM–S Rifle
"Winchester Model 70 Featherweight
"Winchester Model 70 Featherweight Classic

"Winchester Model 70 Featherweight WinTuff
"Winchester Model 70 Lightweight Rifle
"Winchester Model 70 SM Sporter
"Winchester Model 70 Sporter
"Winchester Model 70 Sporter WinTuff
"Winchester Model 70 Stainless Rifle
"Winchester Model 70 Super Express Magnum
"Winchester Model 70 Super Grade
"Winchester Model 70 Synthetic Heavy Varmint
Rifle
"Winchester Model 70 Varmint
"Winchester Ranger Rifle

Centerfire Rifles—Single Shot

"Armsport 1866 Sharps Rifle, Carbine
"Ballard Arms Inc. 1875 #3 Gallery Single Shot Rifle
"Ballard Arms Inc. 1875 #4 Perfection Rifle
"Ballard Arms Inc. 1875 #7 Long Range Rifle
"Ballard Arms Inc. 1875 #8 Union Hill rifle
"Ballard Arms Inc. 1875 11/2 Hunter Rifle
"Ballard Arms Inc. 1885 High Wall Sporting Rifle
"Ballard Arms Inc. 1885 Low Wall Single Shot
"Brown Model 97D Single Shot Rifle
"Brown Model One Single Shot Rifle
"Browning Model 1885 Single Shot Rifle
"C. Sharps Arms 1875 Target & Sporting Rifle
"C. Sharps Arms Custom New Model 1877
"C. Sharps Arms New Model 1885 High Wall Rifle
"C. Sharps Arms 1874 Bridgeport Sporting Rifle

"C. Sharps Arms 1875 Classic Sharps
"C. Sharps Arms New Model 1874 Old Reliable
"C. Sharps Arms New Model 1875 Rifle
"C. Sharps Arms New Model 1875 Target & Long Range
"Cabela's 1874 Sharps Sporting
"Cimarron Billy Dixon 1874 Sharps
"Cimarron Model 1885 High Wall
"Cimarron Quigley Model 1874 Sharps
"Cimarron Silhouette Model 1874 Sharps
"Dakota Model 10 Single Shot Rifle
"Dakota Single Shot Rifle
"Desert Industries G–90 Single Shot Rifle
"Dixie Gun Works 1873 Trapdoor Rifle/Carbine
"Dixie Gun Works 1874 Sharps Rifles
"Dixie Gun Works Remington Rolling Block Rifles
"EMF Premier 1874 Sharps
"Harrington & Richardson Buffalo Classic Rifle (CR–1871)
"Harrington & Richardson CR 45–LC
"Harrington & Richardson Handi-Mag Rifle
"Harrington & Richardson Handi-Rifle
"Harrington & Richardson Handi-Rifle Compact
"Harrington & Richardson New England Hand-Rifle/Slug Gun Combos
"Harrington & Richardson Stainless Handi-Rifle
"Harrington & Richardson Stainless Ultra Hunter Thumbhole Stock
"Harrington & Richardson Superlight Handi-Rifle Compact

"Harrington & Richardson Survivor Rifle
"Harrington & Richardson Synthetic Handi-Rifle
"Harrington & Richardson Ultra Hunter Rifle
"Harrington & Richardson Ultra Varmint Fluted
"Harrington & Richardson Ultra Varmint Rifle
"Harrington & Richardson Ultra Varmint Thumb-
hole Stock
"Krieghoff Hubertus Single Shot
"Meacham High Wall
"Merkel K1 Lightweight Stalking Rifle
"Merkel K2 Custom Stalking Rifle
"Model 1885 High Wall Rifle
"Navy Arms #2 Creedmoor Rifle
"Navy Arms 1873 John Bodine Rolling Black Rifle
"Navy Arms 1873 Springfield Cavalry Carbine
"Navy Arms 1874 Sharps Rifles
"Navy Arms 1874 1885 High Wall Rifles
"Navy Arms Rolling Block Buffalo Rifle
"Navy Arms Sharps "Quigley" Rifle
"Navy Arms Sharps Cavalry Carbine
"Navy Arms Sharps Plains Rifle
"New England Firearms Handi-Rifle
"New England Firearms Sportster/Versa Pack Rifle
"New England Firearms Survivor Rifle
"Red Willow Armory Ballard No. 1.5 Hunting Rifle
"Red Willow Armory Ballard No. 4.5 Target Rifle
"Red Willow Armory Ballard No. 5 Pacific
"Red Willow Armory Ballard No. 8 Union Hill Rifle
"Red Willow Armory Ballard Rifles
"Remington Model Rolling Block Rifles

"Remington Model SPR18 Blued

"Remington Model SPR18 Nickel

"Remington Model SPR18 Single Shot Rifle

"Remington-Style Rolling Block Carbine

"Rossi Match Pairs Rifles

"Rossi Single Shot Rifles

"Rossi Wizard

"Ruger No. 1 RSI International

"Ruger No. 1 Stainless Sporter

"Ruger No. 1 Stainless Standard

"Ruger No. 1A Light Sporter

"Ruger No. 1B Single Shot

"Ruger No. 1H Tropical Rifle

"Ruger No. 1S Medium Sporter

"Ruger No. 1V Special Varminter

"Sharps 1874 Old Reliable

"Shiloh 1875 Rifles

"Shiloh Sharps 1874 Business Rifle

"Shiloh Sharps 1874 Long Range Express

"Shiloh Sharps 1874 Military Carbine

"Shiloh Sharps 1874 Military Rifle

"Shiloh Sharps 1874 Montana Roughrider

"Shiloh Sharps Creedmoor Target

"Thompson/Center Contender Carbine

"Thompson/Center Contender Carbine Survival System

"Thompson/Center Contender Carbine Youth Model

"Thompson/Center Encore

"Thompson/Center Stainless Contender Carbine

"Thompson/Center TCR '87 Single Shot Rifle
"Thompson/Encore Rifles
"Traditions 1874 Sharps Deluxe Rifle
"Traditions 1874 Sharps Standard Rifle
"Traditions Rolling Block Sporting Rifle
"Uberti (Stoeger Industries) Sharps Rifles
"Uberti 1871 Rolling Block Rifle/Carbine
"Uberti 1874 Sharps Sporting Rifle
"Uberti 1885 High Wall Rifles
"Uberti Rolling Block Baby Carbine
"Uberti Springfield Trapdoor Carbine/Rifle

Drillings, Combination Guns, Double Rifles

"A. Zoli Rifle-Shotgun O/U Combo
"Auguste Francotte Boxlock Double Rifle
"Auguste Francotte Sidelock Double Rifles
"Baikal IZH–94 Express
"Baikal MP94– (IZH–94) O/U
"Beretta Express SSO O/U Double Rifles
"Beretta Model 455 SxS Express Rifle
"Chapuis RGExpress Double Rifle
"CZ 584 SOLO Combination Gun
"CZ 589 Stopper O/U Gun
"Dakota Double Rifle
"Garbi Express Double Rifle
"Harrington & Richardson Survivor
"Harrington & Richardson Synthetic Handi-Rifle/
Slug Gun Combo
"Heym Model 55B O/U Double Rifle
"Heym Model 55FW O/U Combo Gun

"Heym Model 88b Side-by-Side Double Rifle
"Hoenig Rotary Round Action Combination Rifle
"Hoenig Rotary Round Action Double Rifle
"Kodiak Mk. IV Double Rifle
"Kreighoff Teck O/U Combination Gun
"Kreighoff Trumpf Drilling
"Krieghoff Drillings
"Lebeau-Courally Express Rifle 5X5
"Merkel Boxlock Double Rifles
"Merkel Drillings
"Merkel Model 160 Side-by-Side Double Rifles
"Merkel Over/Under Combination Guns
"Merkel Over/Under Double Rifles
"Remington Model SPR94 .410/Rimfire
"Remington Model SPR94 12 Gauge/Centerfire
"Rizzini Express 90L Double Rifle
"Savage 24F O/U Combination Gun
"Savage 24F–12T Turkey Gun
"Springfield Inc. M6 Scout Rifle/Shotgun
"Tikka Model 412s Combination Gun
"Tikka Model 412S Double Fire
Rimfire Rifles—Autoloaders

"AMT Lightning 25/22 Rifle
"AMT Lightning Small-Game Hunting Rifle II
"AMT Magnum Hunter Auto Rifle
"Anschutz 525 Deluxe Auto
"Armscor Model 20P Auto Rifle
"Browning Auto .22 Rifles
"Browning Auto-22 Rifle

"Browning Auto-22 Grade VI
"Browning BAR .22 Auto Rifle
"Browning SA–22 Semi-Auto 22 Rifle
"Henry U.S. Survival .22
"Henry U.S. Survival Rifle AR–7
"Krico Model 260 Auto Rifle
"Lakefield Arms Model 64B Auto Rifle
"Marlin Model 60 Self Loading Rifles
"Marlin Model 60C
"Marlin Model 60SB
"Marlin Model 60S–CF
"Marlin Model 60SN
"Marlin Model 60ss Self-Loading Rifle
"Marlin Model 70 Auto-loading Rifles
"Marlin Model 70 HC Auto
"Marlin Model 70P Papoose
"Marlin Model 70PSS
"Marlin Model 795
"Marlin Model 795SS
"Marlin Model 922 Magnum Self-Loading Rifle
"Marlin Model 990l Self-Loading Rifle
"Marlin Model 995 Self-Loading Rifle
"Mossberg 702 Plinkster
"Norinco Model 22 ATD Rifle
"Remington 552BDL Speedmaster Rifle
"Remington Model 522 Viper Autoloading Rifle
"Remington Model 597 Blaze Camo
"Remington Model 597 Pink Camo
"Remington Model 597 Synthetic Scope Combo
"Ruger 10/22 Autoloading Carbine (w/o folding

stock)
"Ruger 10/22 Compact
"Ruger 10/22 Sporter
"Ruger 10/22 Target
"Survival Arms AR–7 Explorer Rifle
"Texas Remington Revolving Carbine
"Thompson/Center R–55 All-Weather
"Thompson/Center R–55 Benchmark
"Thompson/Center R–55 Classic
"Thompson/Center R–55 Rifles
"Thompson/Center R–55 Sporter
"Voere Model 2115 Auto Rifle

Rimfire Rifles—Lever & Slide Action

"Browning BL–22 Lever-Action Rifle
"Henry .22 Lever Action Rifles, All Models
"Henry Golden Boy .17 HMR
"Henry Golden Boy .22
"Henry Golden Boy .22 Magnum
"Henry Golden Boy Deluxe
"Henry Lever .22 Magnum
"Henry Lever Action .22
"Henry Lever Carbine .22
"Henry Lever Octagon .22
"Henry Lever Octagon .22 Magnum
"Henry Lever Youth Model .22
"Henry Pump Action Octagon .22
"Henry Pump Action Octagon .22 Magnum
"Henry Varmint Express .17 HMR

"Marlin 39TDS Carbine
"Marlin Model 39A Golden Lever Action
"Marlin Model 39AS Golden Lever-Action Rifle
"Mossberg Model 464 Rimfire Lever Action Rifle
"Norinco EM–321 Pump Rifle
"Remington 572BDL Fieldmaster Pump Rifle
"Rossi Model 62 SA Pump Rifle
"Rossi Model 62 SAC Carbine
"Rossi Model G2 Gallery Rifle
"Ruger Model 96 Lever-Action Rifle
"Taurus Model 62-Pump
"Taurus Model 72 Pump Rifle
"Winchester Model 9422 Lever-Action Rifle
"Winchester Model 9422 Magnum Lever-Action
Rifle

Rimfire Rifles—Bolt Actions & Single Shots

"Anschutz 1416D/1516D Classic Rifles
"Anschutz 1418D/1518D Mannlicher Rifles
"Anschutz 1700 FWT Bolt-Action Rifle
"Anschutz 1700D Bavarian Bolt-Action Rifle
"Anschutz 1700D Classic Rifles
"Anschutz 1700D Custom Rifles
"Anschutz 1700D Graphite Custom Rifle
"Anschutz 1702 D H B Classic
"Anschutz 1713 Silhouette
"Anschutz Achiever
"Anschutz Achiever Bolt-Action Rifle
"Anschutz All other Bolt Action Rimfire Models

"Anschutz Kadett
"Anschutz Model 1502 D Classic
"Anschutz Model 1517 D Classic
"Anschutz Model 1517 MPR Multi Purpose
"Anschutz Model 1517 S–BR
"Anschutz Model 1710 D KL
"Anschutz Model 1717 Classic
"Anschutz Model 1717 Silhouette Sporter
"Anschutz Model G4 MPB
"Anschutz Model Woodchucker
"Armscor Model 14P Bolt-Action Rifle
"Armscor Model 1500 Rifle
"Beeman/HW 60–J–ST Bolt-Action Rifle
"BRNO ZKM 452 Deluxe
"BRNO ZKM–456 Lux Sporter
"BRNO ZKM–452 Deluxe Bolt-Action Rifle
"Browning A-Bolt 22 Bolt-Action Rifle
"Browning A-Bolt Gold Medallion
"Browning T-Bolt Rimfire Rifles
"Cabanas Espronceda IV Bolt-Action Rifle
"Cabanas Leyre Bolt-Action Rifle
"Cabanas Master Bolt-Action Rifle
"Cabanas Phaser Rifle
"Chipmunk Single Shot Rifle
"Cooper Arms Model 36S Sporter Rifle
"Cooper Model 57–M Bolt Action Rifle
"CZ 452 Bolt Action Rifles
"Dakota 22 Sporter Bolt-Action Rifle
"Davey Crickett Single Shot Rifle
"Harrington & Richardson Sportster

"Harrington & Richardson Sportster 17 Hornady Magnum Rimfire
"Harrington & Richardson Sportster Compact
"Henry 'Mini' Bolt Action Rifle
"Henry Acu-Bolt .22
"Henry Mini Bolt Youth .22
"Kimber Bolt Action .22 Rifles
"Krico Model 300 Bolt-Action Rifles
"Lakefield Arms Mark I Bolt-Action Rifle
"Lakefield Arms Mark II Bolt-Action Rifle
"Magtech Model MT Bolt Action Rifle
"Magtech Model MT–22C Bolt-Action Rifle
"Marlin Model 15YN 'Little Buckaroo'
"Marlin Model 25MN Bolt-Action Rifle
"Marlin Model 25N Bolt-Action Repeater
"Marlin Model 880 Bolt-Action Rifle
"Marlin Model 881 Bolt-Action Rifle
"Marlin Model 882 Bolt-Action Rifle
"Marlin Model 883 Bolt-Action Rifle
"Marlin Model 883SS Bolt-Action Rifle
"Marlin Model 915 YN 'Little Buckaroo'
"Marlin Model 915Y (Compact)
"Marlin Model 915YS (Compact)
"Marlin Model 917
"Marlin Model 917S
"Marlin Model 917V
"Marlin Model 917VR
"Marlin Model 917VS
"Marlin Model 917VS–CF
"Marlin Model 917VSF

"Marlin Model 917VST
"Marlin Model 917VT
"Marlin Model 925
"Marlin Model 925C
"Marlin Model 925M
"Marlin Model 925R
"Marlin Model 925RM
"Marlin Model 980S
"Marlin Model 980S–CF
"Marlin Model 981T
"Marlin Model 982 Bolt Action Rifle
"Marlin Model 982VS
"Marlin Model 982VS–CF
"Marlin Model 983
"Marlin Model 983S
"Marlin Model 983T
"Marlin Model XT–17 Series Bolt Action Rifles
"Marlin Model XT–22 Series Bolt Action Rifles
"Mauser Model 107 Bolt-Action Rifle
"Mauser Model 201 Bolt-Action Rifle
"Meacham Low-Wall Rifle
"Mossberg Model 801/802 Bolt Rifles
"Mossberg Model 817 Varmint Bolt Action Rifle
"Navy Arms TU–33/40 Carbine
"Navy Arms TU–KKW Sniper Trainer
"Navy Arms TU–KKW Training Rifle
"New England Firearms Sportster Single Shot Rifles
"Norinco JW–15 Bolt-Action Rifle
"Norinco JW–27 Bolt-Action Rifle
"Remington 40–XR Rimfire Custom Sporter

"Remington 541–T
"Remington 541–T HB Bolt-Action
"Rifle Remington 581–S Sportsman Rifle
"Remington Model Five
"Remington Model Five Youth
"Rossi Matched Pair Single Shot Rifle
"Ruger 77/17
"Ruger 77/22
"Ruger 77/22 Rimfire Bolt-Action Rifle
"Ruger 77/44
"Ruger K77/22 Varmint Rifle
"Savage CUB T Mini Youth
"Savage Mark I–G Bolt Action
"Savage Mark II Bolt Action Rifles
"Savage Model 30 G Stevens Favorite
"Savage Model 93 Rifles
"Thompson/Center Hotshot Youth Rifle
"Ultra Light Arms Model 20 RF Bolt-Action Rifle
"Winchester Model 52B Sporting Rifle
"Winchester Wildcat Bolt Action Rifle 22

Competition Rifles—Centerfire & Rimfire

"Anschutz 1803D Intermediate Match
"Anschutz 1808D RT Super Match 54 Target
"Anschutz 1827B Biathlon Rifle
"Anschutz 1827BT Fortner Biathlon Rifle
"Anschutz 1903 Rifles
"Anschutz 1903D Match Rifle
"Anschutz 1907 Match Rifle
"Anschutz 1910 Super Match II

"Anschutz 1911 Match Rifle
"Anschutz 1912 Rifles
"Anschutz 1913 Super Match Rifle
"Anschutz 54.18MS REP Deluxe Silhouette Rifle
"Anschutz 54.18MS Silhouette Rifle
"Anschutz 64 MP R Silhouette Rifle
"Anschutz 64–MS Left Silhouette
"Anschutz Super Match 54 Target Model 2007
"Anschutz Super Match 54 Target Model 2013
"Beeman/Feinwerkbau 2600 Target Rifle
"Cooper Arms Model TRP–1 ISU Standard Rifle
"E.A.A./HW 60 Target Rifle
"E.A.A./HW 660 Match Rifle
"E.A.A./Weihrauch HW 60 Target Rifle
"Ed Brown Model 704, M40A2 Marine Sniper
"Finnish Lion Standard Target Rifle
"Krico Model 360 S2 Biathlon Rifle
"Krico Model 360S Biathlon Rifle
"Krico Model 400 Match Rifle
"Krico Model 500 Kricotronic Match Rifle
"Krico Model 600 Match Rifle
"Krico Model 600 Sniper Rifle
"Lakefield Arms Model 90B Target Rifle
"Lakefield Arms Model 91T Target Rifle
"Lakefield Arms Model 92S Silhouette Rifle
"Marlin Model 2000 Target Rifle
"Mauser Model 86–SR Specialty Rifle
"McMillan 300 Phoenix Long Range Rifle
"McMillan Long Range Rifle
"McMillan M–86 Sniper Rifle

"McMillan M–89 Sniper Rifle
"McMillan National Match Rifle
"Parker-Hale M–85 Sniper Rifle
"Parker-Hale M–87 Target Rifle
"Remington 40–X Bolt Action Rifles
"Remington 40–XB Rangemaster Target Centerfire
"Remington 40–XBBR KS
"Remington 40–XC KS National Match Course Rifle
"Remington 40–XR KS Rimfire Position Rifle
"Sako TRG–21 Bolt-Action Rifle
"Sako TRG–22 Bolt Action Rifle
"Springfield Armory M–1 Garand
"Steyr-Mannlicher SSG Rifles
"Steyr-Mannlicher Match SPG–UIT Rifle
"Steyr-Mannlicher SSG P–I Rifle
"Steyr-Mannlicher SSG P–II Rifle
"Steyr-Mannlicher SSG P–III Rifle
"Steyr-Mannlicher SSG P–IV Rifle
"Tanner 300 Meter Free Rifle
"Tanner 50 Meter Free Rifle
"Tanner Standard UIT Rifle
"Time Precision 22RF Bench Rifle
"Wichita Silhouette Rifle

Shotguns—Autoloaders

"American Arms
"American Arms/Franchi Black Magic 48/AL
"Benelli Bimillionaire

"Benelli Black Eagle Competition Auto Shotgun
"Benelli Cordoba
"Benelli Executive Series
"Benelli Legacy Model
"Benelli M1
"Benelli M1 Defense
"Benelli M1 Tactical
"Benelli M1014 Limited Edition
"Benelli M2
"Benelli M2 Field Steady Grip
"Benelli M2 Practical
"Benelli M2 Tactical
"Benelli M2 American Series
"Benelli M3 Convertible
"Benelli M4 Models Vinci Steady Grip
"Benelli Montefeltro Super 90 20-Gauge Shotgun
"Benelli Montefeltro Super 90 Shotgun
"Benelli Raffaello Series Shotguns
"Benelli Sport Model
"Benelli Super 90 M1 Field Model
"Benelli Super Black Eagle II Models
"Benelli Super Black Eagle II Steady Grip
"Benelli Super Black Eagle Models
"Benelli Super Black Eagle Shotgun
"Benelli Super Black Eagle Slug Gun
"Benelli Super Vinci
"Benelli Supersport
"Benelli Two-Gun Sets
"Benelli Ultralight
"Benelli Vinci

"Beretta 390 Field Auto Shotgun
"Beretta 390 Super Trap, Super Skeet Shotguns
"Beretta 3901 Citizen
"Beretta 3901 Rifled Slug Gun
"Beretta 3901 Statesman
"Beretta A–303 Auto Shotgun
"Beretta A400 Series
"Beretta AL–2 Models
"Beretta AL–3 Deluxe Trap
"Beretta AL390 Series
"Beretta AL391 Teknys Gold
"Beretta AL391 Teknys Gold Sporting
"Beretta AL391 Teknys Gold Target
"Beretta AL391 Urika 2 Camo AP
"Beretta AL391 Urika 2 Camo Max-4
"Beretta AL391 Urika 2 Classic
"Beretta AL391 Urika 2 Gold
"Beretta AL391 Urika 2 Gold Sporting
"Beretta AL391 Urika 2 Parallel Target SL
"Beretta AL391 Urika 2 Sporting
"Beretta AL391 Urika 2 Synthetic
"Beretta EH4EAA48F66925464E83F8BEC0AD-C83F4D00 Pintail Series
"Beretta Model 1200 Field
"Beretta Model 1201F Auto Shotgun
"Beretta Model 300
"Beretta Model 301 Series
"Beretta Model 302 Series
"Beretta Model 60
"Beretta Model 61

"Beretta Model A304 Lark
"Beretta Model AL391 Series
"Beretta Model TX4 Storm
"Beretta Silver Lark
"Beretta UGB25 Xcel
"Beretta Vittoria Auto Shotgun
"Beretta Xtrema2
"Breda Altair
"Breda Altair Special
"Breda Aries 2
"Breda Astro
"Breda Astrolux
"Breda Echo
"Breda Ermes Series
"Breda Gold Series
"Breda Grizzly
"Breda Mira
"Breda Standard Series
"Breda Xanthos
"Brolin BL–12
"Brolin SAS–12
"Browning A–500G Auto Shotgun
"Browning A–500G Sporting Clays
"Browning A–500R Auto Shotgun
"Browning Auto-5 Light 12 and 20
"Browning Auto-5 Magnum 12
"Browning Auto-5 Magnum 20
"Browning Auto-5 Stalker
"Browning B2000 Series
"Browning BSA 10 Auto Shotgun

"Browning BSA 10 Stalker Auto Shotgun
"Browning Gold Series
"Browning Maxus Series
"Charles Daly Field Grade Series
"Charles Daly Novamatic Series
"Charles Daly Tactical
"Churchill Regent
"Churchill Standard Model
"Churchill Turkey Automatic Shotgun
"Churchill Windsor
"Cosmi Automatic Shotgun
"CZ 712
"CZ 720
"CZ 912
"Escort Escort Series
"European American Armory (EAA) Bundra Series
"Fabarms Ellegi Series
"Fabarms Lion Series
"Fabarms Tactical
"FNH USA Model SLP
"Franchi 610VS
"Franchi 612 Series
"Franchi 620
"Franchi 712
"Franchi 720
"Franchi 912
"Franchi AL 48
"Franchi AL 48 Series
"Franchi Elite
"Franchi I–12 Inertia Series

"Franchi Prestige
"H&K Model 512
"H&R Manufrance
"H&R Model 403
"Hi-Standard 10A
"Hi-Standard 10B
"Hi-Standard Semi Automatic Model
"Hi-Standard Supermatic Series
"Ithaca Mag-10
"Ithaca Model 51 Series
"LaSalle Semi-automatic
"Ljutic Bi-matic Autoloader
"Luger Ultra-light Model
"Marlin SI 12 Series
"Maverick Model 60 Auto Shotgun
"Model AL–1
"Mossberg 1000
"Mossberg Model 600 Auto Shotgun
"Mossberg Model 930 All-Purpose Field
"Mossberg Model 930 Slugster
"Mossberg Model 930 Turkey
"Mossberg Model 930 Waterfowl
"Mossberg Model 935 Magnum Combos
"Mossberg Model 935 Magnum Flyway Series Wa-
terfowl
"Mossberg Model 935 Magnum Grand Slam Series
Turkey
"Mossberg Model 935 Magnum Turkey
"Mossberg Model 935 Magnum Waterfowl
"New England Firearms Excell Auto Combo

"New England Firearms Excell Auto Synthetic
"New England Firearms Excell Auto Turkey
"New England Firearms Excell Auto Walnut
"New England Firearms Excell Auto Waterfowl
"Nighthawk Tactical Semi-auto
"Ottomanguns Sultan Series
"Remington 105Ti Series
"Remington 1100 20-Gauge Deer Gun
"Remington 1100 LT–20 Auto
"Remington 1100 LT–20 Tournament Skeet
"Remington 1100 Special Field
"Remington 11–48 Series
"Remington 11–96 Series
"Remington Model 105 Cti
"Remington Model 11 Series
"Remington Model 1100 Classic Trap
"Remington Model 1100 Competition
"Remington Model 1100 G3
"Remington Model 1100 G3
"Remington Model 1100 Series
"Remington Model 1100 Shotgun
"Remington Model 1100 Sporting Series
"Remington Model 11–87 Sportsman Camo
"Remington Model 11–87 Sportsman Super Mag
Synthetic
"Remington Model 11–87 Sportsman Super Mag
Waterfowl
"Remington Model 11–87 Sportsman Synthetic
"Remington Model 11–87 Sportsman Youth
"Remington Model 11–87 Sportsman Youth Syn-

thetic

"Remington Model 48 Series

"Remington Model 58 Series

"Remington Model 870 Classic Trap

"Remington Model 878A Automaster

"Remington Model SP–10 Magnum Satin

"Remington Model SP–10 Waterfowl

"Remington Model SPR453

"Remington Versa-Max Series

"Savage Model 720

"Savage Model 726

"Savage Model 740C Skeet Gun

"Savage Model 745

"Savage Model 755 Series

"Savage Model 775 Series

"Scattergun Technologies K–9

"Scattergun Technologies SWAT

"Scattergun Technologies Urban Sniper Model

"SKB 1300 Upland

"SKB 1900

"SKB 300 Series

"SKB 900 Series

"SKS 3000

"Smith & Wesson Model 1000

"Smith & Wesson Model 1012 Series

"Spartan Gun Works SPR453

"TOZ Model H–170

"Tri-Star Diana Series

"Tri-Star Phantom Series

"Tri-Star Viper Series

"Tula Arms Plant TOZ 87
"Verona 401 Series
"Verona 405 Series
"Verona 406 Series
"Verona SX801 Series
"Weatherby Centurion Series
"Weatherby Field Grade
"Weatherby Model 82
"Weatherby SA–08 Series
"Weatherby SA–459 TR
"Weatherby SAS Series
"Winchester 1500
"Winchester Model 50
"Winchester Model 59
"Winchester Super X1 Series
"Winchester Super X2 Series
"Winchester Super X3 Series

Shotguns—Slide Actions

"ADCO Diamond Grade
"ADCO Diamond Series Shotguns
"ADCO Mariner Model
"ADCO Sales Inc. Gold Elite Series
"Armscor M–30 Series
"Armscor M–5
"Baikal IZH–81
"Baikal MP133
"Benelli Nova Series
"Benelli Supernova Series

"Beretta Ariete Standard
"Beretta Gold Pigeon Pump
"Beretta Model SL–12
"Beretta Ruby Pigeon Pump
"Beretta Silver Pigeon Pump
"Brolin Field Series
"Brolin Lawman Model
"Brolin Slug Special
"Brolin Slugmaster
"Brolin Turkey Master
"Browning BPS Game Gun Deer Special
"Browning BPS Game Gun Turkey Special
"Browning BPS Pigeon Grade Pump Shotgun
"Browning BPS Pump Shotgun
"Browning BPS Pump Shotgun (Ladies and Youth
Model)
"Browning BPS Series Pump Shotgun
"Browning BPS Stalker Pump Shotgun
"Browning Model 12 Limited Edition Series
"Browning Model 42 Pump Shotgun
"Century IJ12 Slide Action
"Century Ultra 87 Slide Action
"Charles Daly Field Hunter
"Ducks Unlimited Dinner Guns
"EAA Model PM2
"Escort Field Series
"Fort Worth Firearms GL18
"H&R Pardner Pump
"Hi-Standard Flite-King Series
"Hi-Standard Model 200

"Interstate Arms Model 981
"Interstate Arms Model 982T
"Ithaca Deerslayer II Rifled Shotgun
"Ithaca Model 87 Deerslayer Shotgun
"Ithaca Model 87 Deluxe Pump Shotgun
"Ithaca Model 87 Series Shotguns
"Ithaca Model 87 Supreme Pump Shotgun
"Ithaca Model 87 Turkey Gun
"Magtech Model 586–VR Pump Shotgun
"Maverick Models 88, 91 Pump Shotguns
"Mossberg 200 Series Shotgun
"Mossberg 3000 Pump shotgun
"Mossberg 535 ATS Series Pump Shotguns
"Mossberg Field Grade Model 835 Pump Shotgun
"Mossberg Model 500 All Purpose Field
"Mossberg Model 500 Bantam
"Mossberg Model 500 Bantam Combo
"Mossberg Model 500 Bantam Pump
"Mossberg Model 500 Camo Pump
"Mossberg Model 500 Combos
"Mossberg Model 500 Flyway Series Waterfowl
"Mossberg Model 500 Grand Slam Series Turkey
"Mossberg Model 500 Muzzleloader
"Mossberg Model 500 Muzzleloader Combo
"Mossberg Model 500 Series Pump Shotguns
"Mossberg Model 500 Slugster
"Mossberg Model 500 Sporting Pump
"Mossberg Model 500 Super Bantam All Purpose
Field
"Mossberg Model 500 Super Bantam Combo

"Mossberg Model 500 Super Bantam Slug
"Mossberg Model 500 Super Bantam Turkey
"Mossberg Model 500 Trophy Slugster
"Mossberg Model 500 Turkey
"Mossberg Model 500 Waterfowl
"Mossberg Model 505 Series Pump Shotguns
"Mossberg Model 505 Youth All Purpose Field
"Mossberg Model 535 ATS All Purpose Field
"Mossberg Model 535 ATS Combos
"Mossberg Model 535 ATS Slugster
"Mossberg Model 535 ATS Turkey
"Mossberg Model 535 ATS Waterfowl
"Mossberg Model 835 Regal Ulti-Mag Pump
"Mossberg Model 835 Series Pump Shotguns
"Mossberg Model 835 Ulti-Mag
"Mossberg Turkey Model 500 Pump
"National Wild Turkey Federation (NWTF) Banquet/Guns of the Year
"New England Firearms Pardner Pump Combo
"New England Firearms Pardner Pump Field
"New England Firearms Pardner Pump Slug Gun
"New England Firearms Pardner Pump Synthetic
"New England Firearms Pardner Pump Turkey Gun
"New England Firearms Pardner Pump Walnut
"New England Firearms Pardner Pump-Compact Field
"New England Firearms Pardner Pump-Compact Synthetic
"New England Firearms Pardner Pump-Compact Walnut

"Norinco Model 98 Field Series
"Norinco Model 983
"Norinco Model 984
"Norinco Model 985
"Norinco Model 987
"Orvis Grand Vazir Series
"Quail Unlimited Limited Edition Pump Shotguns
"Remington 870 Express
"Remington 870 Express Rifle Sighted Deer Gun
"Remington 870 Express Series Pump Shotguns
"Remington 870 Express Turkey
"Remington 870 High Grade Series
"Remington 870 High Grades
"Remington 870 Marine Magnum
"Remington 870 Special Field
"Remington 870 Special Purpose Deer Gun
"Remington 870 Special Purpose Synthetic Camo
"Remington 870 SPS Special Purpose Magnum
"Remington 870 SPS–BG–Camo Deer/Turkey Shotgun
"Remington 870 SPS–Deer Shotgun
"Remington 870 SPS–T Camo Pump Shotgun
"Remington 870 TC Trap
"Remington 870 Wingmaster
"Remington 870 Wingmaster Series
"Remington 870 Wingmaster Small Gauges
"Remington Model 11–87 XCS Super Magnum Waterfowl
"Remington Model 870 Ducks Unlimited Series Dinner Pump Shotguns

"Remington Model 870 Express
"Remington Model 870 Express JR.
"Remington Model 870 Express Shurshot Synthetic Cantilever
"Remington Model 870 Express Super Magnum
"Remington Model 870 Express Synthetic
"Remington Model 870 Express Youth Gun
"Remington Model 870 Express Youth Synthetic
"Remington Model 870 SPS Shurshot Synthetic Cantilever
"Remington Model 870 SPS Shurshot Synthetic Turkey
"Remington Model 870 SPS Special Purpose Magnum Series Pump Shotguns
"Remington Model 870 SPS Super Mag Max Gobbler
"Remington Model 870 XCS Marine Magnum
"Remington Model 870 XCS Super Magnum
"Winchester 12 Commercial Riot Gun
"Winchester 97 Commercial Riot Gun
"Winchester Model 12 Pump Shotgun
"Winchester Model 120 Ranger
"Winchester Model 1200 Series Shotgun
"Winchester Model 1300 Ranger Pump Gun
"Winchester Model 1300 Ranger Pump Gun Combo & Deer Gun
"Winchester Model 1300 Series Shotgun
"Winchester Model 1300 Slug Hunter Deer Gun
"Winchester Model 1300 Turkey Gun
"Winchester Model 1300 Walnut Pump

"Winchester Model 42 High Grade Shotgun
"Winchester Speed Pump Defender
"Winchester SXP Series Pump Shotgun
"Zoli Pump Action Shotgun

Shotguns—Over/Unders

"ADCO Sales Diamond Series Shotguns
"American Arms/Franchi Falconet 2000 O/U
"American Arms Lince
"American Arms Silver I O/U
"American Arms Silver II Shotgun
"American Arms Silver Skeet O/U
"American Arms Silver Sporting O/U
"American Arms Silver Trap O/U
"American Arms WS/OU 12, TS/OU 12 Shotguns
"American Arms WT/OU 10 Shotgun
"American Arms/Franchi Sporting 2000 O/U
"Armsport 2700 O/U Goose Gun
"Armsport 2700 Series O/U
"Armsport 2900 Tri-Barrel Shotgun
"AYA Augusta
"AYA Coral A
"AYA Coral B
"AYA Excelsior
"AYA Model 37 Super
"AYA Model 77
"AYA Model 79 Series
"Baby Bretton Over/Under Shotgun
"Baikal IZH27

"Baikal MP310
"Baikal MP333
"Baikal MP94
"Beretta 90 DE LUXE
"Beretta 682 Gold E Skeet
"Beretta 682 Gold E Trap
"Beretta 682 Gold E Trap Bottom Single
"Beretta 682 Series
"Beretta 682 Super Sporting O/U
"Beretta 685 Series
"Beretta 686 Series
"Beretta 686 White Onyx
"Beretta 686 White Onyx Sporting
"Beretta 687 EELL Classic
"Beretta 687 EELL Diamond Pigeon
"Beretta 687 EELL Diamond Pigeon Sporting
"Beretta 687 series
"Beretta 687EL Sporting O/U
"Beretta Alpha Series
"Beretta America Standard
"Beretta AS
"Beretta ASE 90 Competition O/U Shotgun
"Beretta ASE 90 Gold Skeet
"Beretta ASE Gold
"Beretta ASE Series
"Beretta ASEL
"Beretta BL Sereis
"Beretta DT10 Series
"Beretta DT10 Trident EELL
"Beretta DT10 Trident L Sporting

"Beretta DT10 Trident Skeet
"Beretta DT10 Trident Sporting
"Beretta DT10 Trident Trap Combo
"Beretta Europa
"Beretta Field Shotguns
"Beretta Gamma Series
"Beretta Giubileo
"Beretta Grade Four
"Beretta Grade One
"Beretta Grade Three
"Beretta Grade Two
"Beretta Milano
"Beretta Model 686 Ultralight O/U
"Beretta Model SO5, SO6, SO9 Shotguns
"Beretta Onyx Hunter Sport O/U Shotgun
"Beretta Over/Under Field Shotguns
"Beretta Royal Pigeon
"Beretta S56 Series
"Beretta S58 Series
"Beretta Series 682 Competition Over/Unders
"Beretta Silver Pigeon II
"Beretta Silver Pigeon II Sporting
"Beretta Silver Pigeon III
"Beretta Silver Pigeon III Sporting
"Beretta Silver Pigeon IV
"Beretta Silver Pigeon S
"Beretta Silver Pigeon V
"Beretta Silver Snipe
"Beretta Skeet Set
"Beretta SO–1

"Beretta SO–2
"Beretta SO–3
"Beretta SO–4
"Beretta SO5
"Beretta SO6 EELL
"Beretta SO–10
"Beretta SO10 EELL
"Beretta Sporting Clay Shotguns
"Beretta SV10 Perennia
"Beretta Ultralight
"Beretta Ultralight Deluxe
"Bertuzzi Zeus
"Bertuzzi Zeus Series
"Beschi Boxlock Model
"Big Bear Arms IJ–39
"Big Bear Arms Sterling Series
"Big Bear IJ–27
"Blaser F3 Series
"Bosis Challenger Titanium
"Bosis Laura
"Bosis Michaelangelo
"Bosis Wild Series
"Boss Custom Over/Under Shotguns
"Boss Merlin
"Boss Pendragon
"Breda Pegaso Series
"Breda Sirio Standard
"Breda Vega Series
"Bretton Baby Standard
"Bretton Sprint Deluxe

"BRNO 500/501
"BRNO 502
"BRNO 801 Series
"BRNO 802 Series
"BRNO BS–571
"BRNO BS–572
"BRNO ZH–300
"BRNO ZH–301
"BRNO ZH–302
"BRNO ZH–303
"Browning 325 Sporting Clays
"Browning 625 Series
"Browning 725 Series
"Browning B–25 Series
"Browning B–26 Series
"Browning B–27 Series
"Browning B–125 Custom Shop Series
"Browning Citori 525 Series
"Browning Citori GTI Sporting Clays
"Browning Citori Lightning Series
"Browning Citori O/U Shotgun
"Browning Citori O/U Skeet Models
"Browning Citori O/U Trap Models
"Browning Citori Plus Trap Combo
"Browning Citori Plus Trap Gun
"Browning Cynergy Series
"Browning Diana Grade
"Browning Lightning Sporting Clays
"Browning Micro Citori Lightning
"Browning Midas Grade

"Browning Special Sporting Clays
"Browning Sporter Model
"Browning ST–100
"Browning Superlight Citori Over/Under
"Browning Superlight Citori Series
"Browning Superlight Feather
"Browning Superposed Pigeon Grade
"Browning Superposed Standard
"BSA Falcon
"BSA O/U
"BSA Silver Eagle
"Cabela's Volo
"Caprinus Sweden Model
"Centurion Over/Under Shotgun
"Century Arms Arthemis
"Chapuis Over/Under Shotgun
"Charles Daly Country Squire Model
"Charles Daly Deluxe Model
"Charles Daly Diamond Series
"Charles Daly Empire Series
"Charles Daly Field Grade O/U
"Charles Daly Lux Over/Under
"Charles Daly Maxi-Mag
"Charles Daly Model 105
"Charles Daly Model 106
"Charles Daly Model 206
"Charles Daly Over/Under Shotguns, Japanese
Manufactured
"Charles Daly Over/Under Shotguns, Prussian
Manufactured

"Charles Daly Presentation Model
"Charles Daly Sporting Clays Model
"Charles Daly Superior Model
"Charles Daly UL
"Churchill Imperial Model
"Churchill Monarch
"Churchill Premiere Model
"Churchill Regent Trap and Skeet
"Churchill Regent V
"Churchill Sporting Clays
"Churchill Windsor III
"Churchill Windsor IV
"Classic Doubles Model 101 Series
"Cogswell & Harrison Woodward Type
"Connecticut Shotgun Company A. Galazan Model
"Connecticut Shotgun Company A–10 American
"Connecticut Valley Classics Classic Field Water-
fowler
"Connecticut Valley Classics Classic Sporter O/U
"Continental Arms Centaure Series
"Cortona Over/Under Shotguns
"CZ 581 Solo
"CZ Canvasback 103D
"CZ Limited Edition
"CZ Mallard 104A
"CZ Redhead Deluxe 103FE
"CZ Sporting
"CZ Super Scroll Limited Edition
"CZ Upland Ultralight
"CZ Wingshooter

"Dakin Arms Model 170
"Darne SB1
"Darne SB2
"Darne SB3
"Depar ATAK
"Doumoulin Superposed Express
"Ducks Unlimited Dinner Guns/Guns of the Year, Over/Under Models
"Dumoulin Boss Royal Superposed
"E.A.A. Falcon
"E.A.A. Scirocco Series
"E.A.A./Sabatti Falcon-Mon Over/Under
"E.A.A./Sabatti Sporting Clays Pro-Gold O/U
"ERA Over/Under
"Famars di Abbiatico & Salvinelli Aries
"Famars di Abbiatico & Salvinelli Castrone
"Famars di Abbiatico & Salvinelli Dove Gun
"Famars di Abbiatico & Salvinelli Excaliber Series
"Famars di Abbiatico & Salvinelli Jorema
"Famars di Abbiatico & Salvinelli Leonardo
"Famars di Abbiatico & Salvinelli Pegasus
"Famars di Abbiatico & Salvinelli Posiden
"Famars di Abbiatico & Salvinelli Quail Gun
"Famars di Abbiatico & Salvinelli Royal
"Famars di Abbiatico & Salvinelli Royale
"Fausti Boutique Series
"Fausti Caledon Series
"Fausti Class Series
"Ferlib Boss Model
"Finnclassic 512 Series

"Franchi 2004 Trap
"Franchi 2005 Combination Trap
"Franchi Alcione Series
"Franchi Aristocrat Series
"Franchi Black Majic
"Franchi Falconet Series
"Franchi Instict Series
"Franchi Model 2003 Trap
"Franchi Renaissance Series
"Franchi Sporting 2000
"Franchi Undergun Model 3000
"Franchi Veloce Series
"Galef Golden Snipe
"Galef Silver Snipe
"Golden Eagle Model 5000 Series
"Griffon & Howe Black Ram
"Griffon & Howe Broadway
"Griffon & Howe Claremont
"Griffon & Howe Madison
"Griffon & Howe Silver Ram
"Griffon & Howe Superbrite
"Guerini Apex Series
"Guerini Challenger Sporting
"Guerini Ellipse Evo
"Guerini Ellipse Evolution Sporting
"Guerini Ellipse Limited
"Guerini Essex Field
"Guerini Flyaway
"Guerini Forum Series
"Guerini Magnus Series

"Guerini Maxum Series
"Guerini Summit Series
"Guerini Tempio
"Guerini Woodlander
"H&R Harrich #1
"H&R Model 1212
"H&R Model 1212WF
"H&R Pinnacle
"Hatfields Hatfield Model 1 of 100
"Heym Model 55 F
"Heym Model 55 SS
"Heym Model 200
"Holland & Holland Royal Series
"Holland & Holland Sporting Model
"IGA 2000 Series
"IGA Hunter Series
"IGA Trap Series
"IGA Turkey Series
"IGA Waterfowl Series
"K.F.C. E-2 Trap/Skeet
"K.F.C. Field Gun
"Kassnar Grade I O/U Shotgun
"KDF Condor Khan Arthemis Field/Deluxe
"Kimber Augusta Series
"Kimber Marias Series
"Krieghoff K-80 Four-Barrel Skeet Set
"Krieghoff K-80 International Skeet
"Krieghoff K-80 O/U Trap Shotgun
"Krieghoff K-80 Skeet Shotgun
"Krieghoff K-80 Sporting Clays O/U

"Krieghoff K–80/RT Shotguns
"Krieghoff Model 20 Sporting/Field
"Krieghoff Model 32 Series
"Lames Field Model
"Lames Skeet Model
"Lames Standard Model
"Lames California Model
"Laurona Model 67
"Laurona Model 82 Series
"Laurona Model 83 Series
"Laurona Model 84 Series
"Laurona Model 85 Series
"Laurona Model 300 Series
"Laurona Silhouette 300 Sporting Clays
"Laurona Silhouette 300 Trap
"Laurona Super Model Over/Unders
"Lebeau Baron Series
"Lebeau Boss Verres
"Lebeau Boxlock with sideplates
"Lebeau Sidelock
"Lebeau Versailles
"Lippard Custom Over/Under Shotguns
"Ljutic LM–6 Deluxe O/U Shotgun
"Longthorne Hesketh Game Gun
"Longthorne Sporter
"Marlin Model 90
"Marocchi Avanza O/U Shotgun
"Marocchi Conquista Over/Under Shotgun
"Marocchi Conquista Series
"Marocchi Model 100

"Marocchi Model 99
"Maverick HS–12 Tactical
"Maverick Hunter Field Model
"McMillan Over/Under Sidelock
"Merkel 201 Series
"Merkel 2016 Series
"Merkel 2116 EL Sidelock
"Merkel 303EL Luxus
"Merkel Model 100
"Merkel Model 101
"Merkel Model 101E
"Merkel Model 200E O/U Shotgun
"Merkel Model 200E Skeet, Trap Over/Unders
"Merkel Model 200SC Sporting Clays
"Merkel Model 203E, 303E Over/Under Shotguns
"Merkel Model 204E
"Merkel Model 210
"Merkel Model 301
"Merkel Model 302
"Merkel Model 304E
"Merkel Model 310E
"Merkel Model 400
"Merkel Model 400E
"Merkel Model 2000 Series
"Mossberg Onyx Reserve Field
"Mossberg Onyx Reserve Sporting
"Mossberg Silver Reserve Field
"Mossberg Silver Reserve Series
"Mossberg Silver Reserve Sporting
"Norinco Type HL12–203

"Omega Standard Over/Under Model
"Orvis Field
"Orvis Knockabout
"Orvis Premier Grade
"Orvis SKB Green Mountain Uplander
"Orvis Sporting Clays
"Orvis Super Field
"Orvis Uplander
"Orvis Waterfowler
"Pederson Model 1000 Series
"Pederson Model 1500 Series
"Perazzi Boxlock Action Hunting
"Perazzi Competition Series
"Perazzi Electrocibles
"Perazzi Granditalia
"Perazzi Mirage Special Four-Gauge Skeet
"Perazzi Mirage Special Skeet Over/Under
"Perazzi Mirage Special Sporting O/U
"Perazzi MS80
"Perazzi MT–6
"Perazzi MX1/MX2
"Perazzi MX3
"Perazzi MX4
"Perazzi MX5
"Perazzi MX6
"Perazzi MX7 Over/Under Shotguns
"Perazzi MX8/20 Over/Under Shotgun
"Perazzi MX8/MX8 Special Trap, Skeet
"Perazzi MX9 Single Over/Under Shotguns
"Perazzi MX10

"Perazzi MX11
"Perazzi MX12 Hunting Over/Under
"Perazzi MX14
"Perazzi MX16
"Perazzi MX20 Hunting Over/Under
"Perazzi MX28, MX410 Game O/U Shotguns
"Perazzi MX2000
"Perazzi MX2005
"Perazzi MX2008
"Perazzi Sidelock Action Hunting
"Perazzi Sporting Classic O/U
"Perugini Maestro Series
"Perugini Michelangelo
"Perugini Nova Boss
"Pietro Zanoletti Model 2000 Field O/U
"Piotti Boss Over/Under Shotgun
"Pointer Italian Model
"Pointer Turkish Model
"Remington 396 Series
"Remington 3200 Series
"Remington Model 32 Series
"Remington Model 300 Ideal
"Remington Model 332 Series
"Remington Model SPR310
"Remington Model SPR310N
"Remington Model SPR310S
"Remington Peerless Over/Under Shotgun
"Remington Premier Field
"Remington Premier Ruffed Grouse
"Remington Premier Series

"Remington Premier STS Competition
"Remington Premier Upland
"Richland Arms Model 41
"Richland Arms Model 747
"Richland Arms Model 757
"Richland Arms Model 787
"Richland Arms Model 808
"Richland Arms Model 810
"Richland Arms Model 828
"Rigby 401 Sidelock
"Rota Model 650
"Rota Model 72 Series
"Royal American Model 100
"Ruger Red Label O/U Shotgun
"Ruger Sporting Clays O/U Shotgun
"Ruger Woodside Shotgun
"Rutten Model RM 100
"Rutten Model RM285
"S.I.A.C.E. Evolution
"S.I.A.C.E. Model 66C
"S.I.A.C.E. 600T Lusso EL
"San Marco 10-Ga. O/U Shotgun
"San Marco 12-Ga. Wildflower Shotgun
"San Marco Field Special O/U Shotgun
"Sauer Model 66 Series
"Savage Model 242
"Savage Model 420/430
"Sig Sauer Aurora Series
"Sig Sauer SA–3
"Sig Sauer SA–5

"Silma Model 70 Series
"SKB Model 85 Series
"SKB Model 500 Series
"SKB Model 505 Deluxe Over/Under Shotgun
"SKB Model 505 Series
"SKB Model 600 Series
"SKB Model 605 Series
"SKB Model 680 Series
"SKB Model 685 Over/Under Shotgun
"SKB Model 685 Series
"SKB Model 700 Series
"SKB Model 785 Series
"SKB Model 800 Series
"SKB Model 880 Series
"SKB Model 885 Over/Under Trap, Skeet, Sporting Clays
"SKB Model 885 Series
"SKB Model 5600 Series
"SKB Model 5700 Series
"SKB Model 5800 Series
"SKB Model GC–7 Series
"Spartan SPR310/320
"Stevens Model 240
"Stevens Model 512
"Stoeger/IGA Condor I O/U Shotgun
"Stoeger/IGA ERA 2000 Over/Under Shotgun
"Techni-Mec Model 610 Over/Under
"Tikka Model 412S Field Grade Over/Under
"Traditions 350 Series Traditions Classic Field Series

"Traditions Classic Upland Series
"Traditions Gold Wing Series
"Traditions Real 16 Series
"Tri Star Model 330 Series
"Tri-Star Hunter EX
"Tri-Star Model 300
"Tri-Star Model 333 Series
"Tri-Star Setter Model
"Tri-Star Silver Series
"Tri-Star Sporting Model
"TULA 120
"TULA 200
"TULA TOZ34
"Universal 7112
"Universal 7312
"Universal 7412
"Universal 7712
"Universal 7812
"Universal 7912
"Verona 501 Series
"Verona 680 Series
"Verona 702 Series
"Verona LX692 Series
"Verona LX980 Series
"Weatherby Athena Grade IV O/U Shotguns
"Weatherby Athena Grade V Classic Field O/U
"Weatherby Athena Series
"Weatherby Classic Field Models
"Weatherby II, III Classic Field O/Us
"Weatherby Orion II Classic Sporting Clays O/U

"Weatherby Orion II series
"Weatherby Orion II Sporting Clays O/U
"Weatherby Orion III Series
"Weatherby Orion O/U Shotguns
"Winchester Model 91
"Winchester Model 96
"Winchester Model 99
"Winchester Model 101 All Models and Grades
"Winchester Model 1001 O/U Shotgun
"Winchester Model 1001 Series
"Winchester Model 1001 Sporting Clays O/U
"Winchester Model G5500
"Winchester Model G6500
"Winchester Select Series
"Zoli Condor
"Zoli Deluxe Model
"Zoli Dove
"Zoli Field Special
"Zoli Pigeon Model
"Zoli Silver Snipe
"Zoli Snipe
"Zoli Special Model
"Zoli Target Series
"Zoli Texas
"Zoli Z Series
"Zoli Z–90 Series
"Zoli Z-Sport Series

Shotguns—Side By Sides

"Armas Azor Sidelock Model
"ADCO Sales Diamond Series Shotguns
"American Arms Brittany Shotgun
"American Arms Derby Side-by-Side
"American Arms Gentry Double Shotgun
"American Arms Grulla #2 Double Shotgun
"American Arms TS/SS 10 Double Shotgun
"American Arms TS/SS 12 Side-by-Side
"American Arms WS/SS 10
"Arizaga Model 31 Double Shotgun
"Armes de Chasse Sidelock and Boxlock Shotguns
"Armsport 1050 Series Double Shotguns
"Arrieta Sidelock Double Shotguns
"Auguste Francotte Boxlock Shotgun
"Auguste Francotte Sidelock Shotgun
"AYA Boxlock Shotguns
"AYA Sidelock Double Shotguns
"Baikal IZH–43 Series Shotguns
"Baikal MP210 Series Shotguns
"Baikal MP213 Series Shotguns
"Baikal MP220 Series Shotguns
"Baker Gun Sidelock Models
"Baltimore Arms Co. Style 1
"Baltimore Arms Co. Style 2
"Bayard Boxlock and Sidelock Model Shotguns
"Beretta 450 series Shotguns
"Beretta 451 Series Shotguns
"Beretta 452 Series Shotguns
"Beretta 470 Series Shotguns
"Beretta Custom Grade Shotguns

"Beretta Francia Standard
"Beretta Imperiale Montecarlo
"Beretta Model 452 Sidelock Shotgun
"Beretta Omega Standard
"Beretta Side-by-Side Field Shotguns
"Beretta Verona/Bergamo
"Bertuzzi Ariete Hammer Gun
"Bertuzzi Model Orione
"Bertuzzi Venere Series Shotguns
"Beschi Sidelock and Boxlock Models
"Bill Hanus Birdgun Doubles
"Bosis Country SxS
"Bosis Hammer Gun
"Bosis Queen Sidelock
"Boss Robertson SxS
"Boss SxS
"Boswell Boxlock Model
"Boswell Feartherweight Monarch Grade
"Boswell Merlin Sidelock
"Boswell Sidelock Model
"Breda Andromeda Special
"BRNO ZP Series Shotguns
"Brown SxS Shotgun
"Browning B–SS
"Browning B–SS Belgian/Japanese Prototype
"Browning B–SS Sidelock
"Browning B–SS Sporter
"Bruchet Model A
"Bruchet Model B
"BSA Classic

"BSA Royal
"Cabela's ATA Grade II Custom
"Cabela's Hemingway Model
"Casartelli Sidelock Model
"Century Coach SxS
"Chapuis RGP Series Shotguns
"Chapuis RP Series Shotguns
"Chapuis Side-by-Side Shotgun
"Chapuis UGP Round Design SxS
"Charles Daly 1974 Wildlife Commemorative
"Charles Daly Classic Coach Gun
"Charles Daly Diamond SxS
"Charles Daly Empire SxS
"Charles Daly Model 306
"Charles Daly Model 500
"Charles Daly Model Dss Double
"Charles Daly Superior SxS
"Churchill Continental Series Shotguns
"Churchill Crown Model
"Churchill Field Model
"Churchill Hercules Model
"Churchill Imperial Model
"Churchill Premiere Series Shotguns
"Churchill Regal Model
"Churchill Royal Model
"Churchill Windsor Series Shotguns
"Cimarron Coach Guns
"Classic Doubles Model 201
"Classic Clot 1878 Hammer Shotgun
"Cogswell & Harrison Sidelock and Boxlock Shot-

guns
"Colt 1883 Hammerless
"Colt SxS Shotgun
"Connecticut Shotgun Co. Model 21
"Connecticut Shotgun Co. RBL Series
"Continental Arms Centaure
"Crescent SxS Model
"Crucelegui Hermanos Model 150 Double
"CZ Amarillo
"CZ Bobwhite
"CZ Competition
"CZ Deluxe
"CZ Durango
"CZ Grouse
"CZ Hammer Models
"CZ Partridge
"CZ Ringneck
"CZ Ringneck Target
"Dakin Model 100
"Dakin Model 147
"Dakin Model 160
"Dakin Model 215
"Dakota American Legend
"Dakota Classic Grade
"Dakota Classic Grade II
"Dakota Classic Grade III
"Dakota Premier Grade
"Dan Arms Deluxe Field Model
"Dan Arms Field Model
"Darne Sliding Breech Series Shotguns

"Davidson Arms Model 63B
"Davidson Arms Model 69SL
"Davidson Arms Model 73 Stagecoach
"Dumoulin Continental Model
"Dumoulin Etendard Model
"Dumoulin Europa Model
"Dumoulin Liege Model
"E.A.A. SABA
"E.A.A./Sabatti Saba-Mon Double Shotgun
"E.M.F. Model 1878 SxS
"E.M.F. Stagecoach SxS Model
"ERA Quail SxS
"ERA Riot SxS
"ERA SxS
"Famars Boxlock Models
"Famars Castore
"Famars Sidelock Models
"Fausti Caledon
"Fausti Class
"Fausti Class Round Body
"Fausti DEA Series Shotguns
"Ferlib Mignon Hammer Model
"Ferlib Model F VII Double Shotgun
"FN Anson SxS Standard Grade
"FN New Anson SxS Standard Grade
"FN Sidelock Standard Grade
"Fox Higher Grade Models (A–F)
"Fox Sterlingworth Series
"Franchi Airone
"Franchi Astore Series

"Franchi Destino
"Franchi Highlander
"Franchi Sidelock Double Barrel
"Francotte Boxlock Shotgun
"Francotte Jubilee Model
"Francotte Sidelock Shotgun
"Galef Silver Hawk SxS
"Galef Zabala SxS
"Garbi Model 100
"Garbi Model 101 Side-by-Side
"Garbi Model 103A, B Side-by-Side
"Garbi Model 200 Side-by-Side
"Gastinne Model 105
"Gastinne Model 202
"Gastinne Model 353
"Gastinne Model 98
"Gib 10 Gauge Magnum
"Gil Alhambra
"Gil Diamond
"Gil Laga
"Gil Olimpia
"Greener Sidelock SxS Shotguns
"Griffin & Howe Britte
"Griffin & Howe Continental Sidelock
"Griffin & Howe Round Body Game Gun
"Griffin & Howe Traditional Game Gun
"Grulla 217 Series
"Grulla 219 Series
"Grulla Consort
"Grulla Model 209 Holland

"Grulla Model 215
"Grulla Model 216 Series
"Grulla Number 1
"Grulla Royal
"Grulla Super MH
"Grulla Supreme
"Grulla Windsor
"H&R Anson & Deeley SxS
"H&R Model 404
"H&R Small Bore SxS Hammer Gun
"Hatfield Uplander Shotgun
"Henry Atkin Boxlock Model
"Henry Atkin Sidelock Model
"Holland & Holland Cavalier Boxlock
"Holland & Holland Dominion Game Gun
"Holland & Holland Northwood Boxlock
"Holland & Holland Round Action Sidelock
"Holland & Holland Round Action Sidelock Para-
dox
"Holland & Holland Royal Hammerless Ejector
Sidelock
"Holland & Holland Sidelock Shotguns
"Holloway premier Sidelock SxS Model
"Hopkins & Allen Boxlock and Sidelock Models
"Huglu SxS Shotguns
"Husqvarna SxS Shotguns
"IGA Deluxe Model
"IGA Turkey Series Model
"Interstate Arms Model 99 Coach Gun
"Ithaca Classic Doubles Series Shotguns

"Ithaca Hammerless Series
"Iver Johnson Hammerless Model Shotguns
"Jeffery Boxlock Shotguns
"Jeffery Sidelock Shotguns
"K.B.I. Grade II SxS
"Khan Coach Gun
"Kimber Valier Series
"Krieghoff Essencia Boxlock
"Krieghoff Essencia Sidelock
"Lanber Imperial Sidelock
"Laurona Boxlock Models
"Laurona Sidelock Models
"Lefever Grade A Field Model
"Lefever Grade A Skeet Model
"Lefever New
"Lefever Model
"Lefever Nitro Special
"Lefever Sideplate Models
"Leforgeron Boxlock Ejector
"Leforgeron Sidelock Ejector
"Liberty Coach Gun Series
"MacNaughton Sidelock Model
"Malin Boxlock Model
"Malin Sidelock Model
"Masquelier Boxlock Model
"Masquelier Sidelock Model
"Medwell SxS Sidelock
"Merkel Model 8, 47E Side-by-Side Shotguns
"Merkel Model 47LSC Sporting Clays Double
"Merkel Model 47S, 147S Side-by-Sides

"Merkel Model 76E
"Merkel Model 122E
"Merkel Model 126E
"Merkel Model 280 Series
"Merkel Model 360 Series
"Merkel Model 447SL
"Merkel Model 1620 Series
"Merkel Model 1622 Series
"Mossberg Onyx Reserve Sporting
"Mossberg Silver Reserve Field
"Navy Arms Model 100
"Navy Arms Model 150
"Orvis Custom Uplander
"Orvis Field Grade
"Orvis Fine Grade
"Orvis Rounded Action
"Orvis Waterfowler
"Parker Fluid Steel Barrel Models (All Grades)
"Parker Reproductions Side-by-Side
"Pederson Model 200
"Pederson Model 2500
"Perazzi DHO Models
"Perugini Ausonia
"Perugini Classic Model
"Perugini Liberty
"Perugini Regina Model
"Perugini Romagna Gun
"Piotti Hammer Gun
"Piotti King Extra Side-by-Side
"Piotti King No. 1 Side-by-Side Piotti Lunik Side-

by-Side
"Piotti Monaco Series
"Piotti Monte Carlo
"Piotti Piuma Side-by-Side
"Piotti Westlake
"Precision Sports Model 600 Series Doubles
"Premier Italian made SxS Shotguns
"Premier Spanish made SxS Shotguns
"Purdy Best Quality Game Gun
"Remington Model 1900 Hammerless
"Remington Model SPR210
"Remington Model SPR220
"Remington Model SPR220 Cowboy
"Remington Premier SxS
"Richland Arms Co. Italian made SxS Models
"Richland Arms Co. Spanish made SxS Models
"Rigby Boxlock Shotgun
"Rigby Hammer Shotgun
"Rizzini Boxlock Side-by-Side
"Rizzini Sidelock Side-by-Side
"Rossi Overlund
"Rossi Squire
"Rota Model 105
"Rota Model 106
"Rota Model 411 Series
"Royal American Model 600 Boxlock
"Royal American Model 800 Sidelock
"Ruger Gold Label
"SAE Model 209E
"SAE Model 210S

"SAE Model 340X
"Sarasqueta Mammerless Sidelock
"Sarasqueta Model 3 Boxlock
"Sauer Boxlock Model Shotguns
"Sauer Sidelock Model Shotguns
"Savage Fox Model FA–1
"Savage Model 550
"Scott Blenheim
"Scott Bowood
"Scott Chatsworth
"Scott Kinmount
"SIACE Italian made SxS Shotguns
"SKB Model 100
"SKB Model 150
"SKB Model 200
"SKB Model 280
"SKB Model 300
"SKB Model 385
"SKB Model 400
"SKB Model 480
"SKB Model 485
"Smith & Wesson Elite Gold Series Grade I
"Smith & Wesson Elite Silver Grade I
"Smith, L.C. Boxlock Hammerless Shotguns
"Smith, L.C. Sidelock Hammerless Shotguns
"Spartan SPR Series Shotguns
"Stevens Model 311/315 Series
"Stoeger/IGA Uplander Side-by-Side Shotgun
"Taylor's SxS Model
"Tri-Star Model 311

"Tri-Star Model 411 Series
"Ugartechea 10-Ga. Magnum Shotgun
"Universal Double Wing SxS
"Vouzelaud Model 315 Series
"Walther Model WSF
"Walther Model WSFD
"Weatherby Atheana
"Weatherby D'Italia Series
"Weatherby Orion
"Westley Richards Best Quality Sidelock
"Westley Richards Boxlock Shotguns
"Westley Richards Connaught Model
"Westley Richards Hand Detachable Lock Model
"William Douglas Boxlock
"Winchester Model 21
"Winchester Model 24
"Zoli Alley Cleaner
"Zoli Classic
"Zoli Falcon II
"Zoli Model Quail Special
"Zoli Pheasant
"Zoli Silver Hawk
"Zoli Silver Snipe

Shotguns—Bolt Actions & Single Shots

"ADCC Diamond Folding Model
"American Arms Single-Shot
"ARMSCOR 301A
"Armsport Single Barrel Shotgun

"Baikal MP18

"Beretta 471 EL Silver Hawk

"Beretta 471 Silver Hawk

"Beretta Beta Single Barrel

"Beretta MKII Trap

"Beretta Model 412

"Beretta Model FS

"Beretta TR-1

"Beretta TR-1 Trap

"Beretta Vandalia Special Trap

"Browning BT-99 Competition Trap Special

"Browning BT-99 Plus Micro

"Browning BT-99 Plus Trap Gun

"Browning Micro Recoilless Trap Shotgun

"Browning Recoilless Trap Shotgun

"Crescent Single Shot Models

"CZ Cottontail

"Desert Industries Big Twenty Shotgun

"Fefever Long Range Field

"Frigon FS-4

"Frigon FT-1

"Frigon FT-C

"Gibbs Midland Stalker

"Greener General Purpose GP MKI/MKII

"H&R Survivor

"H&R Tracker Slug Model

"Harrington & Richardson N.W.T.F. Turkey Mag

"Harrington & Richardson Pardner

"Harrington & Richardson Pardner Compact

"Harrington & Richardson Pardner Compact Tur-

key Gun
"Harrington & Richardson Pardner Screw-In Choke
"Harrington & Richardson Pardner Turkey Gun
"Harrington & Richardson Pardner Turkey Gun Camo
"Harrington & Richardson Pardner Waterfowl
"Harrington & Richardson Tamer
"Harrington & Richardson Tamer 20
"Harrington & Richardson Topper Classic Youth Shotgun
"Harrington & Richardson Topper Deluxe Classic
"Harrington & Richardson Topper Deluxe Model 098
"Harrington & Richardson Topper Junior
"Harrington & Richardson Topper Model 098
"Harrington & Richardson Topper Trap Gun
"Harrington & Richardson Tracker II Slug Gun
"Harrington & Richardson Ultra Slug Hunter
"Harrington & Richardson Ultra Slug Hunter Compact
"Harrington & Richardson Ultra Slug Hunter Deluxe
"Harrington & Richardson Ultra Slug Hunter Thumbhole Stock
"Harrington & Richardson Ultra-Lite Slug Hunter
"Hi-Standard 514 Model
"Holland & Holland Single Barrel Trap
"IGA Reuna Model
"IGA Single Barrel Classic
"Ithaca Model 66

"Ithaca Single Barrel Trap
"Iver Johnson Champion Series
"Iver Johnson Commemorative Series Single Shot Shotgun
"Iver Johnson Excel
"Krieghoff K–80 Single Barrel Trap Gun
"Krieghoff KS–5 Special
"Krieghoff KS–5 Trap Gun
"Lefever Trap Gun
"Ljutic LTX Super Deluxe Mono Gun
"Ljutic Mono Gun Single Barrel
"Ljutic Recoilless Space Gun Shotgun
"Marlin Model 55 Goose Gun Bolt Action
"Marlin Model 60 Single Shot
"Marocchi Model 2000
"Mossberg Models G–4, 70, 73, 73B
"Mossberg Models 75 Series
"Mossberg Models 80, 83, 83B, 83D
"Mossberg 173 Series
"Mossberg Model 183 Series
"Mossberg Model 185 Series
"Mossberg Model 190 Series
"Mossberg Model 195 Series
"Mossberg Model 385 Series
"Mossberg Model 390 Series
"Mossberg Model 395 Series
"Mossberg Model 595 Series
"Mossberg Model 695 Series
"New England Firearms N.W.T.F. Shotgun
"New England Firearms Standard Pardner

"New England Firearms Survival Gun
"New England Firearms Tracker Slug Gun
"New England Firearms Turkey and Goose Gun
"Parker Single Barrel Trap Models
"Perazzi TM1 Special Single Trap
"Remington 90–T Super Single Shotgun
"Remington Model No. 9
"Remington Model 310 Skeet
"Remington Model No. 3
"Rossi Circuit Judge Lever Action Shotgun
"Rossi Circuit Judge Shotgun
"Ruger Single Barrel Trap
"S.W.D. Terminator
"Savage Kimel Kamper Single Shot
"Savage Model 210F Slug Warrior
"Savage Model 212 Slug Gun
"Savage Model 220 Series
"Savage Model 220 Slug Gun
"SEITZ Single Barrel Trap
"SKB Century II Trap
"SKB Century Trap
"SKB Model 505 Trap
"SKB Model 605 Trap
"Smith, L.C. Single Barrel Trap Models
"Snake Charmer II Shotgun
"Stoeger/IGA Reuna Single Barrel Shotgun
"Tangfolio Model RSG–16
"Tangfolio Blockcard Model
"Tangfolio Model DSG
"Tangfolio Model RSG–12 Series

"Tangfolio Model RSG–20
"Tangfolio RSG-Tactical
"Taurus Circuit Judge Shotgun
"Thompson/Center Encore Shotgun
"Thompson/Center Pro Hunter Turkey Shotgun
"Thompson/Center TCR '87 Hunter Shotgun
"Universal Firearms Model 7212 Single Barrel Trap
"Winchester Model 36 Single Shot
"Winchester Model 37 Single Shot
"Winchester Model 41 Bolt Action
"Winchester Model 9410 Series
"Zoli Apache Model
"Zoli Diano Series
"Zoli Loner Series".

SEC. 513. PENALTIES.

Section 924(a)(1)(B) of title 18, United States Code, is amended by striking "or (q) of section 922" and inserting "(q), (r), (v), (w), or (aa) of section 922".

SEC. 514. USE OF BYRNE GRANTS FOR BUY-BACK PROGRAMS FOR SEMIAUTOMATIC ASSAULT WEAPONS AND LARGE CAPACITY AMMUNITION FEEDING DEVICES.

Section 501(a)(1) of the Omnibus Crime Control and Safe Streets Act of 1968 (42 U.S.C. 3751(a)(1)) is amended by adding at the end the following: "(H) Compensation for surrendered semiautomatic assault weapons and large capacity ammunition feeding devices, as those terms are defined in section 921 of title 18, United States Code, under buy-back programs for semiautomatic assault weapons and large capacity ammunition feeding devices.".

SEC. 515. BAN ON UNTRACEABLE AND UNDETECTABLE FIREARMS.

(a) Requirement That All Firearms Be Traceable.—

(1) DEFINITIONS.—Section 921(a) of title 18, United States Code, as amended by this Act, is amended—

(A) in paragraph (3)—

(i) by inserting ", including an unfinished frame or receiver" after "such weapon"; and

(ii) by striking "or (D) any destructive device" and inserting "; (D) any destructive device; or (E) any combination of parts designed or intended for use in converting any device into a firearm and from which a firearm may be readily assembled";

(B) in paragraph (10), by adding at the end the following: "The term 'manufacturing firearms' includes assembling a functional firearm from a frame or receiver or molding, machining, or 3D printing a frame or receiver, and does not include making or fitting special barrels, stocks, or trigger mechanisms to firearms."; and

(C) by inserting after paragraph (50) the following:
"(51) The term 'frame or receiver'—

"(A) means the part of a firearm that can provide the action or housing for the hammer, bolt, or breechblock and firing mechanism;

"(B) includes a frame or lower receiver blank, casting, or machined body that requires further machining or molding to be used as part of a functional firearm, and which is designed and intended to be used in the assembly of a functional firearm; and

"(C) does not include a piece of material that has had—

"(i) its size or external shape altered solely to facilitate transportation or storage; or

"(ii) solely its chemical composition altered.

"(52) The term 'ghost gun'—

"(A) means a firearm, including a frame or receiver, that lacks a unique serial number engraved or cast in metal or metal alloy on the frame or receiver by a licensed manufacturer or importer in accordance with this chapter; and

"(B) does not include a firearm that has been rendered permanently inoperable.".

(2) PROHIBITION; REQUIREMENTS.—Section 922 of title 18, United States Code, is amended by adding at the end the following:
"(aa) Untraceable Firearms.—

"(1) MANUFACTURE, SALE, OFFER TO SELL, TRANSFER, PURCHASE, OR RECEIPT OF GHOST GUNS.—

"(A) IN GENERAL.—Except as provided in subparagraph (B), it shall be unlawful for any person to manufacture, sell, offer to sell, transfer, purchase, or receive a ghost gun in or affecting interstate or foreign commerce.

"(B) EXCEPTIONS.—Subparagraph (A) shall not apply to—

"(i) the manufacture of a firearm by a licensed manufacturer if the licensed manufacturer complies with section 923(i) before selling or transferring the firearm to another person;

"(ii) the offer to sell, sale, or transfer of a firearm to, or purchase or receipt of a firearm by, a licensed manufacturer or importer before the date that is 1 year after the date of enactment of this subsection;

or

"(iii) a transaction between a licensed manufacturer and a licensed importer on any date.

"(2) SERIAL NUMBERS.—It shall be unlawful for a person other than a licensed manufacturer or importer to engrave or cast a serial number on a firearm in or affecting interstate or foreign commerce.

"(3) POSSESSION OF GHOST GUN WITH INTENT TO SELL, TRANSFER, OR MANUFACTURE.—Beginning on the date that is 1 year after the date of enactment of this subsection, it shall be unlawful for any person other than a licensed manufacturer or importer to possess a ghost gun in or affecting interstate or foreign commerce with the intent to—

"(A) sell or transfer the ghost gun with or without further manufacturing; or

"(B) manufacture a firearm with the ghost gun.".

(3) REQUIREMENTS.—Section 923(i) of title 18, United States Code, is amended by adding at the end the following: "The serial number shall be engraved or cast in metal or metal alloy and sufficient to identify the firearm and the manufacturer or importer that put the serial number on the firearm.".

(4) PENALTIES.—Section 924 of title 18, United States Code, as amended by this Act, is amended—

(A) in subsection (a)(1)(B), by striking "or (w)" and inserting "(w), or (aa)"; and

(B) in subsection (d)(1), by striking "or (k)" and inserting "(k), or (aa)".

(b) Modernization Of The Prohibition On Undetectable Firearms.—Section 922(p) of title 18, United States Code, is amended—

(1) in the matter preceding paragraph (1), by striking "any firearm";

(2) in paragraph (1)—

(A) by striking subparagraph (A) and inserting the following:
"(A) an undetectable firearm; or"; and

(B) in subparagraph (B), by striking "any major component of which, when subjected to inspection by the types of x-ray machines commonly used at airports, does not generate" and inserting the following: "a major component of a firearm which, if subjected to inspection by the types of detection devices commonly used at airports for security screening, would not generate";

(3) by striking paragraph (2) and inserting the following:
"(2) For purposes of this subsection—

"(A) the term 'detectable material' means any material that creates a magnetic field equivalent to or more than 3.7 ounces of 17–4 pH stainless steel;

"(B) the term 'major component', with respect to a firearm—

"(i) means the slide or cylinder or the frame or receiver of the firearm; and

"(ii) in the case of a rifle or shotgun, includes the barrel of the firearm; and

"(C) the term 'undetectable firearm' means a firearm, as defined in section 921(a)(3)(A), of which no major component is wholly made of detectable material;";

(4) in paragraph (3)—

(A) in the first sentence, by inserting ", including a prototype," after "of a firearm"; and

(B) by striking the second sentence; and

(5) in paragraph (5), by striking "shall not apply to any firearm which" and all that follows and inserting the following: "shall not apply to—
"(A) any firearm received by, in the possession of, or under the control of the United States; or

"(B) the manufacture, importation, possession, transfer, receipt, shipment, or delivery of a firearm by a licensed manufacturer or licensed importer pursuant to a contract with the United States.".

SEC. 516. PROHIBITION ON POSSESSION OF CERTAIN FIREARM ACCESSORIES.

Chapter 44 of title 18, United States Code, is amended—

(1) in section 922, as amended by section 515 of this Act, by adding at the end the following:

"(bb) (1) Except as provided in paragraph (2), on and after the date that is 90 days after the date of enactment of this subsection, it shall be unlawful for any person to import, sell, manufacture, transfer, or possess, in or affecting interstate or foreign commerce, a trigger crank, a bump-fire device, or any part, combination of parts, component, device, attachment, or accessory that is designed or functions to materially accelerate the rate of fire of a semiautomatic rifle but not convert the semiautomatic rifle into a machinegun.

"(2) This subsection does not apply with respect to the importation for, manufacture for, sale to, transfer to, or possession by or under the authority of, the United States or any department or agency thereof or a State, or a department, agency, or political subdivision thereof."; and

(2) in section 924(a)(2), by striking ", or (o)" and inserting "(o), or (bb)".

Subtitle B—Firearm Silencers And Mufflers Ban

SEC. 521. DEFINITION.
Section 921(a)(3) of title 18, United States Code, is amended by striking "(C) any firearm muffler or firearm silencer; or (D)" and inserting "or (C)"; and

SEC. 522. RESTRICTIONS ON FIREARM SILENCERS AND FIREARM MUFFLERS.
(a) In General.—Section 922 of title 18, United States Code, as amended by section 516 of this Act, is amended by adding at the end the following:
"(cc) (1) Except as provided in paragraph (2), it shall be unlawful for a person to import, sell, manufacture, transfer, or possess, in or affecting interstate or foreign commerce, a firearm silencer or firearm muffler.

"(2) Paragraph (1) shall not apply to—

"(A) the importation for, manufacture for, sale to, transfer to, or possession by the United States or a department or agency of the United States or a State or a department, agency, or political subdivision of a State, or a sale or transfer to or possession by a qualified law enforcement officer employed by the United States or a department or agency of the United States or a State or a department, agency, or political subdivision of a State for purposes of law enforcement (whether on or off duty), or a sale or transfer to or possession by a campus law enforcement officer for purposes of law enforcement (whether on or off duty);

"(B) the importation for, or sale or transfer to a licensee under title I of the Atomic Energy Act of 1954 (42 U.S.C. 2011 et seq.) for purposes of establishing and maintaining an on-site physical protection system and security organization required by Federal law, or possession by an employee or contractor of such licensee on site for such purposes or off site for purposes of licensee-authorized training or transportation of nuclear materials; or

"(C) the importation for, manufacture for, sale to, transfer to, or possession by a licensed manufacturer or licensed importer for the purposes of testing or experimentation authorized by the Attorney

General.

"(3) For purposes of paragraph (2)(A), the term 'campus law enforcement officer' means an individual who is—

"(A) employed by a private institution of higher education that is eligible for funding under title IV of the Higher Education Act of 1965 (20 U.S.C. 1070 et seq.);

"(B) responsible for the prevention or investigation of crime involving injury to persons or property, including apprehension or detention of persons for such crimes;

"(C) authorized by Federal, State, or local law to carry a firearm, execute search warrants, and make arrests; and

"(D) recognized, commissioned, or certified by a government entity as a law enforcement officer.".

(b) Seizure And Forfeiture Of Firearm Silencers And Firearm Mufflers.—Section 924(d) of title 18, United States Code, as amended by section 512(d) of this Act, is amended—

(1) in paragraph (1), by striking "or (w)" and inserting "(w), or (cc)"; and

(2) in paragraph (3)(E), by inserting "922(cc)," after "922(w),".

SEC. 523. PENALTIES.

Section 924(a)(1)(B) of title 18, United States Code, as amended by section 513 of this Act, is amended by striking "or (w)" and inserting "(w), or (cc)".

SEC. 524. EFFECTIVE DATE.

The amendments made by this subtitle shall take effect on the date that is 90 days after the date of enactment of this Act.

TITLE VI—FIREARM TRAFFICKING

SEC. 601. PROHIBITION AGAINST MULTIPLE FIREARM SALES OR PURCHASES.

(a) Prohibition.—Section 922 of title 18, United States Code, as amended by this Act, is amended by adding at the end the following:

"(dd) Prohibition Against Multiple Firearm Sales Or Purchases.—

"(1) SALE.—It shall be unlawful to sell, transfer, or otherwise dispose of a firearm, in of affecting interstate or foreign commerce, to any person who is not licensed under section 923 knowing or having reasonable cause to believe that such person purchased a firearm during the 30-day period ending on the date of such sale or disposition.

"(2) PURCHASE.—It shall be unlawful for any person who is not licensed under section 923 to purchase more than 1 firearm that has been shipped or transported in interstate or foreign commerce during any 30-day period.

"(3) EXCEPTIONS.—Paragraphs (1) and (2) shall not apply to—

"(A) a lawful exchange of 1 firearm for 1 firearm;

"(B) the transfer to or purchase by the United States, a department or agency of the United States, a State, or a department, agency, or political subdivision of a State, of a firearm;

"(C) the transfer to or purchase by a law enforcement officer employed by an entity referred to in subparagraph (B) of a firearm for law enforcement purposes (whether on or off duty);

"(D) the transfer to or purchase by a rail police officer employed by a rail carrier and certified or commissioned as a police officer under the laws of a State of a firearm for law enforcement purposes (whether on or off duty); or

"(E) the transfer or purchase of a firearm listed as a

curio or relic by the Attorney General pursuant to section 921(a)(13).".

(b) Penalties.—Section 924(a)(2) of title 18, United States Code, as amended by this Act, is amended by striking "or (cc)" and inserting "(cc), or (dd)".

(c) Conforming Amendments.—Chapter 44 of title 18, United States Code, is amended—

(1) in section 922(s), as so redesignated by section 201 of this Act—

(A) in paragraph (1)(B)(ii), by striking "(g) or (n)" and inserting "(g), (n), or (dd)(2)";

(B) in paragraph (2), by striking "(g) or (n)" and inserting "(g), (n), or (dd)(2)";

(C) in paragraph (4), by striking "(g) or (n)" and inserting "(g), (n), or (dd)(2)"; and

(D) in paragraph (5), by striking "(g) or (n)" and inserting "(g), (n), or (dd)(2)"; and

(2) in section 925A, by striking "(g) or (n)" and inserting "(g), (n), or (dd)(2)".

(d) Eliminate Multiple Sales Reporting Requirement.—Section 923(g) of title 18, United States

Code, is amended by striking paragraph (3).

(e) Authority To Issue Rules And Regulations.—The Attorney General shall prescribe any rules and regulations as are necessary to ensure that the national instant criminal background check system is able to identify whether receipt of a firearm by a prospective transferee would violate section 922(dd) of title 18, United States Code, as added by this Act.

SEC. 602. INCREASED PENALTIES FOR MAKING KNOWINGLY FALSE STATEMENTS IN CONNECTION WITH FIREARMS.

Section 924(a)(3) of title 18, United States Code, is amended in the matter following subparagraph (B) by striking "one year" and inserting "5 years".

SEC. 603. RETENTION OF RECORDS.

Section 922(s)(2) of title 18, United States Code, as so redesignated by section 201 of this Act, is amended—

(1) in subparagraph (B), by striking "; and" and inserting a period; and

(2) by striking subparagraph (C).

SEC. 604. REVISED DEFINITION.

Section 921(a)(21)(C) of title 18, United States Code, is amended by inserting ", except that such term shall include any person who transfers more than 1 firearm in any 30-day period to a person who is not a licensed dealer" before the semicolon.

SEC. 605. FIREARMS TRAFFICKING.

(a) In General.—Chapter 44 of title 18, United States Code, as amended by section 402 of this Act, is amended by adding at the end the following:

"§ 934. Trafficking in firearms

"(a) Offenses.—It shall be unlawful for any person, regardless of whether anything of value is exchanged—

"(1) to ship, transport, transfer, or otherwise dispose to a person, 2 or more firearms in or affecting interstate or foreign commerce, if the transferor knows or has reasonable cause to believe that such shipping, transportation, transfer, or disposition of the firearm would be in violation of, or would result in a violation of any Federal, State, or local law punishable by a term of imprisonment exceeding 1 year;

"(2) to receive from a person, 2 or more firearms in or affecting interstate or foreign commerce, if the recipient knows or has reasonable cause to believe that such receipt would be in violation of, or would result in a violation of any Federal, State, or local law punishable by a term of imprisonment exceeding 1 year;

"(3) to make a statement to a licensed importer, licensed manufacturer, or licensed dealer relating to the purchase, receipt, or acquisition from a licensed importer, licensed manufacturer, or licensed dealer of 2 or more firearms that have moved in or affected interstate or foreign commerce that—

"(A) is material to—

"(i) the identity of the actual buyer of the firearms; or

"(ii) the intended trafficking of the firearms; and

"(B) the person knows or has reasonable cause to believe is false; or

"(4) to direct, promote, or facilitate conduct specified in paragraph (1), (2), or (3).

"(b) Penalties.—

"(1) IN GENERAL.—Any person who violates, or conspires to violate, subsection (a) shall be fined under this title, imprisoned for not more than 15 years, or both.

"(2) ORGANIZER ENHANCEMENT.—If a violation of subsection (a) is committed by a person in concert with 5 or more other persons with respect to whom such person occupies a position of organizer, a supervisory position, or any other position of management, such person may be sentenced to an additional term of imprisonment of not more than 5 consecutive years.

"(c) Definitions.—In this section—

"(1) the term 'actual buyer' means the individual for whom a firearm is being purchased, received, or acquired; and

"(2) the term 'term of imprisonment exceeding 1 year' does not include any offense classified by the applicable jurisdiction as a misdemeanor and punishable by a term of imprisonment of 2 years or less.".

(b) Technical And Conforming Amendment.—The table of sections for chapter 44 of title 18, United States Code, as amended by section 402 of this Act, is amended by adding at the end the following:

"934. Trafficking in firearms.".

TITLE VII—DEALER REFORM

SEC. 701. GUN SHOP SECURITY MEASURES.

(a) Regulations.—

(1) IN GENERAL.—Section 926 of title 18, United States Code, is amended by adding at the end the following:

"(d) Not later than 1 year after the date of enactment of this subsection, the Attorney General shall prescribe such regulations as are necessary to ensure that any premises at which a licensed dealer deals in firearms are secure from theft, which shall include requiring—

"(1) compliance with the security plan submitted by the licensed dealer pursuant to section 923(d)(1)(G);

"(2) the use of locked metal cabinets and fireproof safes;

"(3) security systems, video monitoring, and anti-theft alarms;

"(4) security gates, strong locks, and site hardening; and

"(5) concrete bollards and other access controls, if necessary.".

(2) TRANSITION RULE.—The regulations prescribed under section 926(d)(1) of title 18, United

States Code, shall not apply to a person who, on the date of enactment of this Act, is a licensed dealer, as defined in section 921(a)(11) of title 18, United States Code, until the earlier of—

(A) the date the person complies with subsection (b)(2) of this section; or

(B) the end of the 1-year period that begins with the date regulations are prescribed under section 926(d) of title 18, United States Code.

(b) Security Plan Submission Requirement And Other Requirements.—

(1) IN GENERAL.—Section 923(d)(1) of title 18, United States Code, is amended by striking sub-paragraph (G) and inserting the following:
"(G) in the case of an application to be licensed as a dealer, the applicant certifies that—

"(i) the applicant has a permanent place of business;

"(ii) the applicant only hires individuals 21 years of age or older as employees; and

"(iii) secure gun storage or safety devices will be available at any place in which firearms are sold under the license to persons who are not licensees (subject to the exception that in any case in which a secure gun storage or safety device is temporarily unavailable because of theft, casualty loss, consumer sales, backorders from a manufacturer, or any other similar reason beyond the control of the licensee, the dealer shall not be considered to be in violation of the requirement under this subparagraph to make available such a device) and include with the certification—

"(I) a description of how the applicant will secure, in accordance with the regulations issued under section 926(d), the premises from which the applicant will conduct business under the license (including in the event of a natural disaster or other emergency); and

"(II) a certification that the applicant, if issued such a license, the applicant will comply with the certification made under this subparagraph.".

(2) TRANSITION RULE.—A person who, on the date of enactment of this Act, is a licensed dealer (as defined in section 921(a)(11) of title 18, United States Code) and whose license to deal in firearms, issued under chapter 44 of title 18, will not expire before the end of the 1-year period beginning on the date on which regulations are prescribed under section 926(d) of title 18, United States Code, shall submit to the Attorney General a plan of the type described in section 923(d)(1)(G) of title 18, Unit-

ed States Code, not later than the end of that 1-year period. Any plan so submitted shall be considered to be submitted pursuant to section 923(d)(1)(G) of title 18, United States Code, for purposes of sections 923(g)(6)(B) and 926(d) of title 18, United States Code.

(c) Annual Security Plan Compliance Certification Requirement.—

(1) IN GENERAL.—Section 923 of title 18, United States Code, is amended by adding at the end the following:
"(m) (1) Each licensed dealer shall annually certify to the Attorney General that each premises from which the licensed dealer conducts business subject to license under this chapter is in compliance with the regulations prescribed under section 926(d), and include with the certification the results of a reconciliation of the firearms inventory of the licensed dealer with the firearms inventory at the time of the most recent prior certification (if any) under this paragraph, including a report of any missing firearms.

"(2) With respect to a violation of paragraph (1), the Attorney General may, after notice and opportunity for a hearing—

"(A) suspend, until the violation is corrected, the

license issued to the licensee under this chapter that was used to conduct the firearms transfer; and

"(B) impose a civil money penalty of not more than $5,000 on a licensed dealer who fails to comply with paragraph (1).".

(2) TRANSITION RULE.—The amendment made by paragraph (1) of this subsection shall not apply to a person who, on the date of enactment of this Act, is a licensed dealer (as defined in section 921(a)(11) of title 18, United States Code), until the end of the 1-year period that begins with the date person complies with subsection (b)(2) of this section.

(d) Effective Date.—The amendments made by this section shall take effect 1 year after the date of enactment of this Act.

SEC. 702. INSPECTIONS.

(a) Elimination Of Limit On Annual Inspections Of Licensees.—Section 923(g)(1)(B)(ii) of title 18, United States Code, is amended—

(1) by striking the em dash and all that follows through "(II)"; and

(2) by striking "licensee." and inserting "licensee".

(b) Mandated Annual Inspections Of High Risk

Licensed Dealers, Triennial Inspections Of Other Licensed Dealers.—Section 923(g)(1) of title 18, United States Code, is amended by adding at the end the following:

"(E) (i) The Attorney General shall, without such reasonable cause or warrant—

"(I) annually inspect or examine the inventory, records, and business premises of each licensed dealer whom the Attorney General determines is a high-risk dealer (based on the considerations used to do so as of the date of the enactment of this sentence); and

"(II) triennially inspect or examine the inventory, records, and business premises of any other licensed dealer that the Attorney General determines is not a high-risk dealer.

"(ii) Not later than 180 days after the date of an inspection under this subparagraph reveals a violation of this section or any regulation prescribed under this chapter, the Attorney General shall conduct an inspection to determine whether such violation has been cured.".

(c) Authority To Hire Additional Industry Operation Investigators For ATF.—

(1) IN GENERAL.—The Attorney General may hire

650 industry operation investigators for the Bureau of Alcohol, Tobacco, Firearms and Explosives, in addition to any personnel needed to carry out this title and the amendments made by this title.

(2) AUTHORIZATION OF APPROPRIATIONS.—There are authorized to be appropriated to the Attorney General such sums as are necessary to carry out paragraph (1).

SEC. 703. EMPLOYEE BACKGROUND CHECKS.

(a) Requirements.—

(1) BACKGROUND CHECK REQUIRED BEFORE FIREARM POSSESSION BY DEALER EMPLOYEE.—Section 923(g) of title 18, United States Code, as amended by section 709 of this Act, is amended by adding at the end the following:

"(10) A licensed dealer may not allow an employee of the licensed dealer to possess a firearm at a premises from which the licensed dealer conducts business subject to license under this chapter unless—

"(A) the licensed dealer has contacted the national instant criminal background check system established under section 103 of the Brady Handgun Violence Prevention Act for information about whether it would be unlawful for the individual to receive a firearm; and

"(B) the system has notified the licensee that the information available to the system does not demonstrate that the receipt of a firearm by the individual would violate subsection (g) or (n) of section 922 or State law.".

(2) BACKGROUND CHECKS REQUIRED BEFORE ISSUANCE OR RENEWAL OF DEALER LICENSE.—Section 923(c) of title 18, United States Code, is amended by inserting after the 1st sentence the following: "Notwithstanding the preceding sentence, the Attorney General may not issue or renew a license to deal in firearms unless the Attorney General has contacted the national instant criminal background check system established under section 103 of the Brady Handgun Violence Prevention Act for information about whether it would be unlawful for any employee of the applicant for the license or renewal, identified by the applicant as having the responsibility to receive a firearm, for information about whether it would be unlawful for the employee to receive a firearm, and the system has notified the Attorney General that the information available to the system does not demonstrate that the receipt of a firearm by the employee would violate subsection (g) or (n) of section 922 or the law of the State in which the business premises of the applicant subject to the license is located.".

(3) EFFECTIVE DATE.—The amendments made by this subsection shall take effect on the date that is 1 year after the date of enactment of this Act.

(b) Authority Of NICS System To Respond To Licensed Dealer Request For Criminal Background Check Of Employee Or Prospective Employee.— Section 103(b) of the Brady Handgun Violence Prevention Act (34 U.S.C. 40901(b)) is amended by adding at the end the following: "The Attorney General shall ensure that the system responds to any request received by the system from a licensed dealer for information on whether receipt of a firearm by an employee or prospective employee of the licensed dealer would violate such section 922 or State law.".

SEC. 704. GUN STORE THEFTS.

Section 923(g)(6) of title 18, United States Code, is amended—

(1) by inserting "(A)" after "(6)"; and

(2) by adding at the end the following:

"(B) (i) Not later than 30 days after the date on which the Attorney General receives a report from a licensed dealer pursuant to subparagraph (A) of this paragraph of the theft of a firearm, the Attorney General shall conduct an independent inspection of the security of the premises at which the theft occurred, which may include an inspection of the measures taken to implement the security plan submitted by the licensed dealer pursuant to subsection (d)(1)(G).

"(ii) On completion of the security inspection, the Attorney General shall provide the licensed dealer with—

"(I) a notice of any violation by the licensed dealer of any security requirements prescribed under section 926(d); and

"(II) recommendations for improving security of the premises involved.

"(iii) Not later than 180 days after the date on which the Attorney General conducts an investigation under this subparagraph that reveals a violation of any security requirement prescribed under section 926(d), the Attorney General shall conduct another investigation to determine whether the violation has been cured.".

SEC. 705. CIVIL ENFORCEMENT.

Section 923 of title 18, United States Code, as amended by section 701(c)(1) of this Act, is amended by adding at the end the following:
"(n) In the case of a licensed dealer who the Attor-

ney General has found to be in violation of a regulation prescribed under this chapter, to not have implemented a corrective action required by the Attorney General at the completion of a security inspection conducted under subsection (g)(6)(B)(i) of this section within 30 days after the date of the inspection, or to be in violation of subsection (g)(8) of this section—

"(1) the Attorney General shall—

"(A) if the violation is not a result of gross negligence by the licensed dealer—

"(i) in the case of the 1st such violation of the law or regulation by the licensed dealer, if not preceded by a violation to which subparagraph (B) applies, transmit to the licensed dealer a written notice specifying the violation, which shall include a copy of the provision of law or regulation violated and a plan for how to cure the violation;

"(ii) in the case of the 2nd such violation by the licensed dealer, if not preceded by a violation to which subparagraph (B) applies, impose a civil money penalty in an amount that is not less than $2,500 and not more than $20,000;

"(iii) in the case of the 3rd such violation by the licensed dealer, if not preceded by a violation to which subparagraph (B) applies, suspend the license to deal in firearms issued to the licensed dealer under this chapter until the violation ceases;

"(iv) in the case of the 4th such violation by the licensed dealer, whether or not preceded by a violation to which subparagraph (B) applies, revoke that license; or

"(v) in the case of any such violation by the licensed dealer, if preceded by a violation to which subparagraph (B) applies, apply the penalty authorized under this subsection that is 1 level greater in severity than the level of severity of the penalty most recently applied to the licensed dealer under this subsection; or

"(B) if the violation is a result of such gross negligence—

"(i) in the case of the 1st such violation by the licensed dealer, impose a civil money penalty in an amount that is not less than $2,500 and not more than $20,000;

"(ii) in the case of the 2nd such violation by the licensed dealer—

"(I) impose a civil money penalty in an amount equal to $20,000; or

"(II) suspend the license to deal in firearms issued to the licensed dealer under this chapter until the violation ceases; or

"(III) revoke that license; or

"(iii) in the case of the 3rd or subsequent such violation by the licensed dealer, apply the penalty authorized under this subsection that is 1 or 2 levels greater in severity than the level of severity of the penalty most recently applied to the licensed dealer under this subsection; and

"(2) in the case of any such violation, if the Attorney General finds that the nature of the violation indicates that the continued operation of a firearms business by the licensed dealer presents an imminent risk to public safety, the Attorney General shall, notwithstanding paragraph (1), immediately suspend the license to deal in firearm issued to the licensed dealer under this chapter and secure the firearms inventory of the licensed dealer, until the violation ceases.".

SEC. 706. NO EFFECT ON STATE LAWS GOVERNING DEALING IN FIREARMS.

Nothing in this title shall be interpreted to preclude a State from imposing or enforcing any requirement relating to dealing in firearms (as defined in section

921(a)(3) of title 18, United States Code).

SEC. 707. LOST AND STOLEN REPORTING REQUIREMENT.

(a) In General.—Section 922 of title 18, United States Code, as amended by section 601 of this Act, is amended by adding at the end the following:
"(ee) The owner of a firearm shall report the theft or loss of the firearm, not later than 48 hours after the owner becomes aware of the theft or loss, to the Attorney General and to the appropriate local authorities.".

(b) Civil Penalty.—Section 924 of title 18, United States Code, is amended by adding at the end the following:
"(q) Whoever violates section 922(ee) shall be fined not more than $1,000 in a civil proceeding.".

SEC. 708. REPORT ON IMPLEMENTATION.

Not later than 2 years after the date of enactment of this Act, the Attorney General shall submit to the Congress a written report on the implementation of this Act and the amendments made by this title, including any remaining steps that are necessary to complete the implementation, which shall also identify any additional resources that are required to conduct regular inspections and to ensure that this title and the amendments made by this title are enforced against noncompliant firearm dealers in a timely manner.

SEC. 709. ENHANCED RECORD KEEPING REQUIREMENTS.

Section 923(g) of title 18, United States Code, is amended by adding at the end the following:

"(8) (A) Each licensed dealer, manufacturer, and importer shall maintain a record of each sale or other transfer of a firearm or ammunition.

"(B) The record required to be maintained under subparagraph (A) shall include—

"(i) the full name, gender, residence, and occupation of the transferee;

"(ii) a complete description of the firearm, including the make, serial number, and type, if applicable;

"(iii) the type of transfer, such as whether the firearm was sold, rented, or leased;

"(iv) the date of transfer; and

"(v) the firearm license number of the transferee issued in accordance with section 932.

"(C) Each record required to be maintained under subparagraph (A) shall be maintained indefinitely and shall, not later than 5 business days after the sale or other transfer, be submitted to the Bureau of Alcohol, Tobacco, Firearms and Explosives.

"(9) Not later than 2 years after the date of enactment of the Gun Violence Prevention and Community Safety Act of 2020, the Attorney General, acting through the Director of the Bureau of Alcohol, Tobacco, Firearms and Explosives, shall establish and maintain an electronic database for the receipt and storing of all records created by licensed dealers under paragraph (8).".

SEC. 710. DEADLINE FOR ISSUANCE OF FINAL REGULATIONS.

Not later than 1 year after the date of enactment of this Act, the Attorney General shall prescribe, in final form, all regulations required to carry out this title and the amendments made by this title.

SEC. 711. REPEAL.

(a) Consolidated Appropriations Resolution, 2003.—Section 644 of title VI of division J of the Consolidated Appropriations Resolution, 2003 (5 U.S.C. 552 note) is amended by striking "or any other Act with respect to any fiscal year".

(b) Consolidated Appropriations Act, 2005.—Title I of division B of the Consolidated Appropriations Act, 2005 (Public Law 108–447; 118 Stat. 2859) is amended in the matter under the heading "SALA-

RIES AND EXPENSES" under the heading "Bureau Of Alcohol, Tobacco, Firearms, And Explosives" under the heading "DEPARTMENT OF JUSTICE" in the 6th proviso by striking "with respect to any fiscal year".

(c) Science, State, Justice, Commerce, And Related Agencies Appropriations Act, 2006.—Title I of the Science, State, Justice, Commerce, and Related Agencies Appropriations Act, 2006 (Public Law 109–108; 119 Stat. 2295) is amended in the matter under the heading "SALARIES AND EXPENSES" under the heading "Bureau Of Alcohol, Tobacco, Firearms, And Explosives" under the heading "DE-PARTMENT OF JUSTICE" in the sixth proviso by striking "with respecting to any fiscal year".

(d) Consolidated Appropriations Act, 2008.—Title II of division B of the Consolidated Appropriations Act, 2008 (Public Law 110–161; 121 Stat. 1903) is amended in the matter under the heading "SALA-RIES AND EXPENSES" under the heading "Bureau Of Alcohol, Tobacco, Firearms, And Explosives" under the heading "DEPARTMENT OF JUSTICE" in the sixth proviso by striking "beginning in fiscal year 2008 and thereafter" and inserting "in fiscal year 2008".

(e) Omnibus Appropriations Act, 2009.—Title II of division B of the Omnibus Appropriations Act,

2009 (Public Law 111–8; 123 Stat. 574) is amended in the matter under the heading "SALARIES AND EXPENSES" under the heading "Bureau Of Alcohol, Tobacco, Firearms, And Explosives" under the heading "DEPARTMENT OF JUSTICE" in the sixth proviso by striking "beginning in fiscal year 2009 and thereafter" and inserting "in fiscal year 2009".

(f) Consolidated Appropriations Act, 2010.—Title II of division B of the Omnibus Appropriations Act, 2009 (Public Law 111–117; 123 Stat. 3128) is amended in the matter under the heading "SALARIES AND EXPENSES" under the heading "Bureau Of Alcohol, Tobacco, Firearms, And Explosives" under the heading "DEPARTMENT OF JUSTICE" in the sixth proviso, by striking "beginning in fiscal year 2010 and thereafter" and inserting "in fiscal year 2010".

(g) Consolidated And Furthering Continuing Appropriations Act, 2012.—Division B of the Consolidated and Furthering Continuing Appropriations Act, 2012 (Public Law 112–55; 125 Stat. 552) is amended—

(1) in title II, in the matter under the heading "SALARIES AND EXPENSES" under the heading "Bureau Of Alcohol, Tobacco, Firearms, And Explosives" under the heading "DEPARTMENT OF

JUSTICE" by striking—

(A) the first proviso;

(B) the sixth proviso; and

(C) the eighth proviso; and

(2) in title V, by striking section 511(2).

(h) Commerce, Justice, Science, And Related Agencies Appropriations Act, 2013.—The Commerce, Justice, Science, and Related Agencies Appropriations Act, 2013 (Division B of Public Law 113–6; 127 Stat. 198) is amended in title II, in the matter under the heading "SALARIES AND EXPENSES" under the heading "Bureau Of Alcohol, Tobacco, Firearms, And Explosives" under the heading "DEPARTMENT OF JUSTICE" by striking—

(1) the first proviso;

(2) the fifth proviso; and

(3) the sixth proviso.

(i) Commerce, Justice, Science, And Related Agencies Appropriations Act, 2019.—The Commerce, Justice, Science, and Related Agencies Appropriations Act, 2019 (Division C of Public Law 116–6;

133 Stat. 91) is amended in title V by striking—

(1) section 517; and

(2) section 531.

TITLE VIII—INDUSTRY REFORM

SEC. 801. REPEAL.
Sections 2, 3, and 4 of the Protection of Lawful Commerce in Arms Act (15 U.S.C. 7901, 7902, and 7903) are repealed.

SEC. 802. REPEAL OF EXCLUSION OF PISTOLS, REVOLVERS, AND OTHER FIREARMS FROM CONSUMER PRODUCT SAFETY LAWS.
(a) Amending The Definition Of Consumer Product.—Section 3(a)(5) of the Consumer Product Safety Act (15 U.S.C. 2052(a)(5)) is amended—

(1) by striking subparagraph (E);

(2) by redesignating subparagraphs (F) through (I) as subparagraphs (E) through (H), respectively; and

(3) in the matter following subparagraph (H) (as redesignated by paragraph (2)), by striking "described in subparagraph (E) of this paragraph or".

(b) Removing Prohibition Of Rulemaking Authority.—Subsection (e) of section 3 of the Consumer Product Safety Commission Improvements Act of 1976 (15 U.S.C. 2080 note) is repealed.

SEC. 803. INCREASE IN EXCISE TAXES RELATING TO FIREARMS.

(a) In General.—Section 4181 of the Internal Revenue Code of 1986 is amended to read as follows:

"SEC. 4181. IMPOSITION OF TAX.

"There is hereby imposed upon the sale by the manufacturer, producer, or importer of the following articles a tax equivalent to the specified percent of the price for which so sold:

"(1) Articles taxable at 30 percent:

"(A) Pistols.

"(B) Revolvers.

"(C) Firearms (other than pistols and revolvers).

"(D) Any lower frame or receiver for a firearm, whether for a semiautomatic pistol, rifle, or shotgun that is designed to accommodate interchangeable upper receivers.

"(2) Articles taxable at 50 percent: Shells and cartridges.".

(b) Exemption For United States.—Subsection (b) of section 4182 of the Internal Revenue Code of 1986 is amended to read as follows:
"(b) Sales To United States.—No firearms, pistols, revolvers, lower frame or receiver for a firearm, shells, and cartridges purchased with funds appropriated for any department, agency, or instrumentality of the United States shall be subject to any tax imposed on the sale or transfer of such articles.".

(c) Effective Date.—The amendments made by this section shall apply with respect to sales after September 30, 2020.

(d) Use Of Increased Taxes.—

(1) USE FOR GUN VIOLENCE PREVENTION AND RESEARCH.—An amount equal to 39 percent of revenues accruing from any tax imposed on shells and cartridges by section 4181 of the Internal Revenue Code of 1986, shall, subject to the exemptions in section 4182 of such title, be covered into the Community Violence Intervention Fund in the Treasury (hereinafter referred to as the "Fund") and is authorized to be appropriated and made available until expended to carry out the purposes of paragraph (2).

(2) PROGRAMS FOR GUN VIOLENCE PREVENTION AND RESEARCH.—Amounts in the Fund established under paragraph (1) shall be used by the Secretary of Health and Human Services to carry out the program established under section 399V–7 of the Public Health Service Act (as added by section 901 of this Act).

(3) CONFORMING AMENDMENT.—

(A) IN GENERAL.—Section 3(a)(1) of the Pittman-Robertson Wildlife Restoration Act (16 U.S.C. 669b (a)(1)) is amended by inserting "(other than 39 percent of the revenues accruing from the taxes imposed on shells and cartridges by section 4181 of such Code)" after "Internal Revenue Code of 1986".

(B) EFFECTIVE DATE.—The amendment made by this paragraph shall apply with respect to sales after September 30, 2020.

TITLE IX—RESEARCH AND COMMUNITY VIOLENCE INTERVENTION PROGRAM

SEC. 901. COMMUNITY VIOLENCE INTERVENTION GRANT PROGRAM.

Part P of title III of the Public Health Service Act (42 U.S.C. 280g et seq.) is amended by adding at the end the following:

"SEC. 399V–7. COMMUNITY VIOLENCE INTERVENTION GRANT PROGRAM.

"(a) In General.—The Secretary shall award grants to eligible entities to support community violence intervention programs, with an emphasis on evidence-informed intervention strategies to reduce homicides, shootings, and group-related violence.

"(b) Eligible Entities.—

"(1) IN GENERAL.—To be eligible for a grant under this section, an entity—

"(A) shall be a local governmental, hospital, or non-profit, community-based organization; and

"(B) submit an application at such time, but not more frequently than biennially, in such manner, and containing—

"(i) clearly defined and measurable objectives for the grant;

"(ii) a statement describing how the applicant proposes to use the grant to implement an evidence-informed violence reduction initiative in accordance with this section; and

"(iii) evidence indicating that the proposed violence

reduction initiative would likely reduce the incidence of homicides, shootings, and group-related violence; and

"(iv) any other information the Secretary may require.

"(2) REQUIRED DISTRIBUTION.—Each local government that receives a grant shall distribute no less than 50 percent of the grant funds to one or more of any of the following types of entities:

"(A) A community-based organization.

"(B) A nonprofit organization.

"(C) A public agency or department, other than a law enforcement agency or department, that is primarily dedicated to community safety or violence prevention.

"(c) Program Activities.—A program supported by a grant under this section—

"(1) shall focus on interrupting cycles of violence by focusing intervention resources on the individuals identified as being at highest risk for being victims or perpetrators of community violence in the near future; and

"(2) shall be used to support, expand, and replicate evidence-informed violence reduction initiatives, including—

"(A) hospital-based violence intervention programs;

"(B) evidence-informed street outreach programs;

"(C) focused deterrence strategies;

"(D) conflict mediation;

"(E) delivery of needs-based support services for high-risk individuals and their family members; and

"(F) providing intensive case management, counseling or peer support services that reduce individuals' risk of being victimized by, or perpetrating, violence and that seek to interrupt cycles of violence and retaliation in order to reduce the incidence of homicides, shootings, and group-related violence.

"(d) Priority.—In awarding grants under this section, the Secretary shall give priority to programs operating in—

"(1) the 127 municipalities that have had the highest annual per capita homicide rates as measured over the most recent 5 years (among municipalities meeting certain population thresholds, as specified by the Secretary); and

"(2) other municipalities with substantial recent increases in homicide rates, based on homicide data reported to the Federal Bureau of Investigation, or as otherwise specified by the Secretary.

"(e) Grant Recipient Reports.—Each recipient of a grant under this section shall submit a biennial performance report to the Secretary detailing how such grant funds were used and the progress made towards addressing violence in the community during the applicable funding period under the grant.

"(f) Reports To Congress.—Not later than 2 years after the date on which the program under this section commences, and every 2 years thereafter, the Secretary shall submit a report to Congress detailing how funds appropriated for the grant program under this section were used and recommendations for improvement of the program.

"(g) Authorization Of Appropriations.—There are authorized to be appropriated to the Secretary to carry out this section $100,000,000 for each fiscal year.".

SEC. 902. FUNDING FOR RESEARCH ON FIRE-

ARMS SAFETY OR GUN VIOLENCE PREVENTION.

(a) Department Of Justice.—

(1) IN GENERAL.—There are authorized to be appropriated to the Attorney General $50,000,000 for each fiscal year for the purpose of conducting or supporting research on firearms safety or gun violence prevention. The amount authorized to be appropriated by the preceding sentence is in addition to any other amounts authorized to be appropriated for such purpose.

(2) REPORTS TO CONGRESS.—Not later than 2 years after the date of enactment of this Act, and every 2 years thereafter, the Attorney General shall submit a report to Congress detailing how the funds authorized to be appropriated under this section were used.

(b) Department Of Health And Human Services.—

(1) IN GENERAL.—There are authorized to be appropriated to the Secretary of Health and Human Services $50,000,000 for each fiscal year for the purpose of conducting or supporting research on firearms safety or gun violence prevention, including conducting evaluations of the community violence intervention grant program authorized under section 399V–7 of the Public Health Service Act

(as added by section 901 of this Act). The amount authorized to be appropriated by the preceding sentence is in addition to any other amounts authorized to be appropriated for such purpose.

(2) REPORTS TO CONGRESS.—Not later than 2 years after the date of enactment of this Act, and every 2 years thereafter, the Secretary of Health and Human Services shall submit a report to Congress detailing how the funds authorized to be appropriated under this section were used.

TITLE X—MISCELLANEOUS

SEC. 1001. SEVERABILITY.

If any provision of this Act or any amendment made by this Act, or any application of such provision or amendment to any person or circumstance, is held to be invalid, the remainder of the provisions of this Act and the amendments made by this Act and the application of the provision or amendment to any other person or circumstance shall not be affected.

Coronavirus Aid, Relief, and Economic Security Act H. R. 748

The CARES Act is the largest spending bill in the history of the United States. Signed into law by President Donald Trump on March 27, 2020, this $2.2 trillion bill appropriates money to help the United States recover from the impacts of COVID-19 (the coronavirus). Read the contents of the bill to learn how the money was allocated.

Gun Violence Prevention and Community Safety Act of 2020 H.R.5717

This bill makes various changes to the federal framework governing the sale, transfer, and possession of firearms and ammunition. It includes a licensing requirement for all firearms, restricts firearm types and capacities, removes civil liabilities, and creates so-called Red Flag laws for teh confiscation of legally owned firearms.

Take Responsibility for Workers and Families Act H.R.6379

Read the overview, summary, and the complete text of the Democratic plan to recover from the COVID-19 crisis. The bill, H.R. 6379 contains substantial spending for multiple sectors of the economy. This bill also includes items unrelated to addressing the financial and life impacts of the crisis.

The FBI Confidential Source Failure by U.S. Department of Justice

Read the Office of the Inspector General's report on the FBI's deficiencies in its handling of classified human sources. This Inspector General identified multiple areas that the Federal Bureau of Investigation failed to properly vet confidential secret sources used for investigation. The Inspector discovered that FBI analysts were pressured into not identifying red flags about these sources, possibly tainting the counterintelligence investigation of the Trump campaign. This information was used to secure warrants for monitoring Trump campaign officials.

The Clinton Email Server Report by U.S. State Department

The U.S. Justice Department assigned Robert Mueller and a team of agents in the spring of 2017 to investigate accusations of collusion between President Donald Trump and Russian operatives. This is the complete text of the declassified, redacted report.

The Mueller Report by Robert Mueller

The U.S. Justice Department assigned Robert Mueller and a team of agents in the spring of 2017 to investigate accusations of collusion between President Donald Trump and Russian operatives. This is the complete text of the declassified, redacted report.

The dude ranch world of Struthers Burt was a romantic destination in the early twentieth century. They transported people back to the Wild West. These ranches were and still are popular destinations. Experience the old west through this dude rancher's writing.

Journeys to the Edge by Randall Peeters, Ph.D.

What is it like to climb Mount Everest? Is it possible for you to actually make the ascent? It requires dreaming big and creating a personal vision to climb the mountains in your life. Randall Peeters shares his successes and failures and gives you some directly applicable guidelines on how you can create a vision for your life.

Lost at Windy Corner by Aaron Linsdau

Windy Corner on Denali has claimed lives, fingers, and toes. What would make someone brave lethal weather, crevasses, and slick ice to attempt to summit North America's highest mountain? The author shares the lessons Denali teaches on managing goals and risks. Apply the message to build resilience and overcome adversity.

Sagebrush Alley by Patricia Jones

What's worse than having a stalker? Being pursued by a second one who has already killed. Attempting to complete her studies, Dana Cameron has to avoid becoming a murder victim. She becomes tangled in a struggle for life trapped in a claustrophobic nightmare.

Sleeping Dogs Don't Lie by Michael McCoy

A young Native American boy is taken from his home after tragedy strikes, grows up in middle America, and through his first real adult summer searches for Wyoming artifacts, falls in with the subversive Dog Soldiers Resurrected, and attempts single-handedly to solve the mystery behind the murder of his treasured coworker.

So I Said by Gerry Spence

The collected sayings of Gerry Spence prods readers into thinking about their own vision of the world. As a lawyer with decades of experience in defending the defenseless, he's fought against giants. His insights provide a grander vision of how the nearly invisible world of the justice system in *So I Said*.

The Burqa Cave by Dean Petersen

Still haunted by Iraq, Tim Ross finds solace teaching high school in Wyoming. That is, until freshman David Jenkins reveals the murder of a lost local girl. Will Tim be able to overcome his demons to stop the murderer?

Voices at Twilight by Lori Howe, Ph.D.

Voices at Twilight is a guide that takes readers on a visual tour of twelve past and present Wyoming ghost towns. Contained within are travel directions, GPS coordinates, and tips for intrepid readers.www.sastrugipress.com

Do you enjoy classic literature? Sastrugi Press has a classic series just for you. Visit our webpage and find more quality books like this one at www.sastrugipress.com/classics/.

Visit Sastrugi Press on the web at www.sastrugipress.com to purchase the above titles in bulk. They are also available from your local bookstore or online retailers in print, e-book, or audiobook form. Thank you for choosing Sastrugi Press.

www.sastrugipress.com

"Turn the Page Loose"

www.ingramcontent.com/pod-product-compliance
Lightning Source LLC
Chambersburg PA
CBHW072213150726

48002CB00005B/1786